RAMBLINGS

Anthony Holbourn

.

DEDICATION
To my older sister and oldest friend, Shelagh,
and to the dearest lady of my later life, Gwen.

ACKNOWLEDGMENTS

I would like to thank Wendy Gifkins, who was seminal in the vision of this volume and the midwife in its parturition; three sons, Tom, Ben and Alex, who have been part of its subsequent growth. All the good friends mentioned by name herein and those implied but not named: they know who they are. To all of these I am grateful for helping devise this surprising and unexpected outcome.

AA

Education failure

If you have ever failed, especially in some part of your education, so be it. If you have sound human qualities, such as trust, truth, honesty, generosity, idiocy, benignity and a readiness to accept confidently whatever turns up, then you will probably cope. In my case it has occurred to me, through the questioning of a curious young granddaughter, that I should try to dig it all up. It is clear that the more you remember, the more you think; and the more you think, the more you remember, as places, pictures, people arise from the past, from the layers of mental wallpaper overlapping each other inside your head.

It would be possible to recount a complete life. However, since this needs to be readable, it is better to select scenes and experiences which avoid tedium. We have, after all, only a lifetime. These reminiscences of a year or so in my life after school and before squeezing through to apparent respectability are not particularly coherent, though they are more so after consulting my editorial team with their sharp, alert and constructive advice, as well as their encouragement.

Auntie Alice

Mum was strongly influenced by her Auntie Alice. We knew her from our earliest years: she was of course our Great-Aunt Alice. We had a number of Great Aunts: Maud, a lofty, haughty woman about whom I remember nothing beyond her manner, sweeping into a room like a galleon under full sail; but AA, as we always called her, was the centre of it all, dignified, friendly and interested.

AA had retired from teaching when I was one year old, so I knew her forever. She was very correct and highly educated and expected nothing less of us. My big sister Shelagh and I used to stay every summer on the south coast, she with our Grandma, Mum's mother, in Polegate near Eastbourne, and I with AA in Saltdean, along the coast from Rottingdean. Every year when we were staying there, we used to take buses and meet in Seaford, halfway between the two, and have tea with these two venerable sisters.

AA lived in her retirement in a bungalow – 3 Arlington Gardens – and it was here I used to stay, year after year. How did I get there? Probably Dad drove me down there, but it was from Polegate, I think, that he whizzed down one year after I innocently told him that there was blood in my urine. It is easy now to see why he was panic-stricken and drove at great speed to Great Ormond Street hospital in London, the leading children's hospital for miles. They took lots of tests but above all I remember staying in there for six weeks, never feeling ill or that I needed to be there. Some pictures remain. Someone brought me a toy helicopter whose rotor blades revolved at speed. On one occasion I and another boy wound it up and I can remember us both looking out of a window as it dropped like a stone to the ground, a little dusty yard six floors below. It was so disappointing! I had expected it to fly, being six years old. AA and I used to take the bus to Brighton every now and again, always to watch the annual Ice Show, always to walk along the piers – for there were two then, the Palace Pier and the West Pier. The latter was never up to much, a bit posh for us and further along towards Hove, but we enjoyed the various attractions on the rather rowdy Palace Pier, especially the Ghost Train with its great, beckoning phantom, the funfair with its helter-skelter and bumper cars, the penny in the slot machines and just walking up and down looking at the sea between the boards or over the light blue rusty railings at the rusty iron girders, all encrusted with barnacles.

Every evening we used to play games. The most memorable was Mah-Jongg: AA had a set of Mah-Jongg playing cards and we used to play for hours. It was only much later that I found out that it was usually played with tiles and that 'Mah-Jongg' was something to do with the sound the tiles made as they were shuffled against each other. Was it the sound of birds? I still have the Mah-Jongg cards and I opened the box only today. There inside were the little score sheets we used to keep sixty years ago, still with our initials and scores in pencil, and the complex set of rules, with the four little packs of cards, Winds, Dragons, Characters and Circles.

Perhaps more impressive was her dark brown china cabinet which adorned the wall opposite the fireplace. She used it for something else, I can't remember what – probably books. It was so much a part of her room that it was a joy when, in her will, I found that she had bequeathed it to me. I still have it now and it has reverted to its original use as a china cabinet. Yes! And I have some of the books as well, multiple volumes of nature, trees, birds. They were more a treasure trove than books to look at and they are as good as new.

AA was always very clear-headed. She had a sort of friend who became increasingly familiar in her later years. One day, in the middle of a conversation, she said to AA, 'And if you were thinking of leaving anything to me in your will…'

'I'm not,' replied AA – and she never saw the woman again.

The third item I still have of AA's is a ring. It is gold, good rich gold, with three-leafed clover or shamrock patterns engraved into it, so that it was reputed to be made of Irish gold, if there is such a thing. It belonged to AA's father and he was wearing it – the story goes – when he was on his way to America, emigrating, and was shipwrecked. This may be an amalgamation of several tales but it is a good one.

Another story that AA used to tell was of when she lived in Beckenham long ago. The great and impressive Crystal Palace had been built to house the Great Exhibition of 1851. There it stood, a vast glass structure with a cast-iron frame, until 1936. I do not know why it burnt down. AA was in her mid-30's then and she told of seeing the molten glass flowing down Sydenham Hill.

Crystal Palace Park still exists and still holds the great statues of dinosaurs which were constructed, I suppose, at the same time. We used to make family expeditions to go and see them.

Early education, Gravesend

We lived in Valley Drive, part of a long road in a council estate. I can remember no names of friends but have a very clear picture of sitting on the window sill of the front upstairs bedroom window, looking down at the grass and uncultivated ground below. There was no particular reason for jumping out – it just seemed interesting. No damage was done, even to the garden.

Shelagh and I used to walk the mile or so to school and back every day, up to Echo Square and down a small hill to the school. There were school dinners, which I loathed and could not eat, though we were not allowed to leave the table until our plates were clean. I used to smother the meals in salt.

We lived our early family life first in our grandmother's house – Dad's mother – then in the council house in Valley Drive. Shelagh and I were sent to the local Catholic junior school – The Convent Prep School in Old Road East. We used to walk there and back, a mile or so each way, up Whitehill Road with its alternate pink and white paving stones, to Echo Square, then turned right.

It was run by The Sisters of Mercy, in their long black habits with hard, almost plastic, white hoods. They were variable in teaching skills. I remember one in particular who taught me something I have never forgotten.

'Now today we're going to learn a poem by Walter Dellermar –' that was how she read De La Mare – 'It's called 'Someone Came Knocking.' We learnt it and performed the actions, cupping our ears, peering this way and that and shaking our heads in bewilderment:

> *'Someone came knocking at my wee,*
> *small door.*
> *Someone came knocking, I'm sure, I'm*
> *sure, I'm sure,*
> *I listened, I opened, I looked to left and*
> *right,*
> *But naught there was a-stirring in the*
> *still, dark night...'*

It was a younger version of the sinister verses *'The Traveller'*:

> *'Is there anybody there?' said the*
> *Traveller,*
> *Knocking on the moonlit door,*
> *And his horse in the silence champed the*
> *grasses*
> *Of the forest's ferny floor.*
> *And a bird flew up out of the turret*
> *Above the Traveller's head,*
> *And he smote upon the door a second*
> *time:*
> *'Is there anybody there?', he said.*
> *But no-one descended to the Traveller,*

No head from the leaf-fringed sill
Peered over and looked into his grey
eyes
Where he stood, perplexed and still ...'

The pictures filled my mind with dark, impossible questions – echoing life in many ways. And the vocabulary! Does anyone 'smite' anything now? The 'leaf-fringed sill' with some calm and indistinguishable face, frightening in its knowing intensity. The last piece I was learning before we moved was 'Hiawatha's Wedding Feast' but it never stuck.

The Sisters were not themselves well educated but my parents – probably our father – felt that it was the best course for us. He himself had been a non-believer, or possibly an Anglican, for years until he met a man called Tony Costelloe in the navy right at the end of the war. They became very good friends since they were both thinkers, talkers and open-minded. Tony had always been a Catholic and through the conversations they had it became obvious to Dad that this was where he had to go instead of being a rather woolly Anglican without much thinking; that was the way he had been brought up. He read Hilaire Belloc and G. K. Chesterton at length and was overwhelmed with the certainty that there was nowhere else to go. Accordingly, he became a Catholic, though I don't know when – probably in the early 1950's.

Kenley and Purley: John Fisher

Later we moved to Kenley in Surrey, not much of a place. Indeed, nowhere we lived could really be called a place. There we owned two cats, Whiskey and Ginger. Ginger disappeared one day and we hunted all round the roads, knocking on neighbours' doors in despair. Nothing. Astonishingly, six months later he re-appeared, probably having lived all that time in the spinney down the road. Then there was Mrs Galloway next door who brewed wine out of anything. I remember the pea-pod wine and the tea wine.

We moved to a house in Purley, Graham Road, I think. You could look through the railings at the end of the road into the fields of the Orphanage and we could hear constantly the sound of trains on the Brighton line a mile away.

This was quite a big house – four bedrooms, I think – but we may have been short of furniture. I do remember having an obsession with the colour yellow and asking if I could have my bedroom painted in 'golden yellow'. The parents were happy enough to let me do it. In the bedroom was the old kitchen cabinet, a tall set of cupboards with a table that pulled out. I used to make towns out of Plasticene on this table, making the bricks with my fingers and laying down the courses, correctly overlapping for strength. There were building sites as well where I had an excuse for not finishing the houses or putting rooves on them. Roads were laid out with Plasticene kerbs and these were populated by my Matchbox cars. I could never mix the latter with any other cars because everything had to be on the same scale.

There was a fashion then for covering up floorboards with hardboard; I wonder why? Since this was not a difficult task, I was given the job of both cutting up the hardboard and nailing it down. How well I remember the lovely, open, smooth feeling of a room freshly boarded, fixed with shiny orange panel pins! I used to lie on my back pretending to be a boat, sliding all round the room, powered by my legs. This meant travelling backwards, making it hazardous, but thoughtlessly I slid at some speed into the tiled surround of the fireplace, all mottled brown and white. The skin on my scalp split and I had to go to Purley hospital.

A few months later I was hurtling down the steps, late for the bus to school – the 234? No, the 197, to change in the town centre – when I tripped and my head came into contact violently with a protruding flint at the side of the steps. Off to hospital again, saved from serious damage by my thick blue school cap. I can see the flint now with its sharp, protruding half-inch. There was a third occasion of head damage but I cannot recall the reason, only the long-suffering sighs from the hospital out-patients' staff when I was brought in again. Doubtless now my parents would be referred to Social Services and had their roles put under scrutiny.

These head injuries might have been the cause of my later head issues but I have always supposed not.

'Did you ever have a head injury when you were a child?' asked hospital staff in neurological departments while investigating my epilepsy 20 years later. I told them, but they could see no connection, since any problems would probably have started much sooner. Epilepsy usually starts in late childhood or adolescence, they say, and mine did not start until I was 28, long after I stopped sliding about on floors.

John Fisher School

I had been sent to the John Fisher preparatory school. John Fisher – not 'Saint John Fisher': he had not been canonised when the school was founded – was a Catholic grammar school. Presumably the 'Prep' school had to be paid for. I was there for a couple of years and learned some French there, taught by a gentle, courteous and clear man called Mr Thompson. Alas, he died of cancer a few years later – the first person I can remember dying. Anyway, it seemed that I was good at learning things and always did what I was told, having no interest in revolution and trusting both parents and authorities.

At the Gravesend convent we had every week to undertake something called 'memory work'. You were given things you simply had to learn by heart, which has been helpful ever since. It made you think about the words and the rhymes, the shape of the verses on the page – it was always verse, not prose – the sounds, and it meant that I was prepared for just learning things, regardless of what they were or why I had to do it. I am sure that people everywhere had to learn that skill and it is a great loss to hear that children do not commit things to memory as much – though I do not know for certain and they must have other ways of enriching their minds.

There was an entrance exam for the grammar school and I did not pass, so that I ought to have gone to the secondary-modern school. As we shall see, I was never very good at exams, despite the English Progress Papers my parents bought to help me prepare. However, it seemed I was on the fringe of passing and my exam performance must have shown some hint of competence and I was asked to attend an interview.

The interview panel were kind, wise and obviously knew everything. They asked questions.

'What would you like to do when you grow up?'

'I'd like to travel.'

'And where would you like to go?'

'Australia, I think.' It just seemed a long way away and interesting, full of kangaroos and deserts, and I could speak English there.

'Right. And how would you get there?'

This was unexpected. However, one of my idle pastimes had always been gazing at maps and atlases so I told them. 'Well, first I would go up to the Thames. Then I would get on a boat and sail down to the Thames Estuary.' Gravesend was on the estuary: from our house two miles from the river, we would hear the tooting of the tugs on the Thames at night. 'Then at the end I would turn right and go into the channel, down the channel to the end ...' it was a little hazy here: France did not appear in my perception '...then left round Spain and into the Mediterranean.' I couldn't remember details of the Mediterranean but knew what to do next. 'Then I would go through the Suez Canal and down Africa, then turn left past India and through some seas...' I was nearly there, more or less. This grasp of world maps evidently did the trick.

It is perhaps surprising that later at school, Geography was a subject I hated and despised, probably because of the teachers; but the trouble was undoubtedly that it was all mixed up with Economics, with land production, with producing 'dot maps' showing the concentration of sheep here and there; it was not about maps. One of the finest things I ever produced at school was a map of the UK showing all the geological strata of the country. It was called 'Geology and Geomorphology' and I had copied it meticulously from an encyclopaedia we had at home. I learned from it the way that beneath the visible soil, all sorts of rocks formed the foundation of the British Isles. I can visualise now the great sweeps of yellows, browns and assorted greens with which it was decorated and clarified.

The other picture in my Geography book was of the

South East of England and its structure. You could see it, a sort of slice – the North and South Downs, with the Weald in between and two other lower lengths of hill called Greensand Ridges, though I don't know where they are. It was clear that the whole area was like a giant saucer with the two sets of hills.

Latin and other things

When we started Latin at the age of 11 the priest who taught us was obnoxious. We just did what he told us, from our brown Shorter Latin Primer – modified on each cover to 'A Shorter way of Eating Prime Beef' in scruffy pen.

'Right. For Monday you will learn the pronoun *is, ea, id*. You will learn it forwards, backwards, sideways, backwards and sideways, so that you can visualise it on the page.

We did this with all the Latin pronouns, with not the smallest idea why, with the verbs and participles and declensions, so that we were well schooled but hated the incomprehensible process. Understanding why you did things was not part of the education process: you just did it, because you trusted the teachers, who obviously knew far more than you did. There were two boys who always did better than me and always would – not that I was the third best, but among the group who were next after the clever ones – but it was a world in which I was more or less comfortable because it brought success through knowing how to learn tables, regardless of how well I could apply the knowledge.

When we entered the fourth year – what you would call year 10 now – we had Fr Fawcett as our Latin teacher, a tall, slender, hawkish priest. He was a revelation. 'It's quite simple. A participle is a *Nadjective*. A *Nadjective*.'

I never knew this before, though I knew what adjectives were and how they worked but it opened my eyes, for he was so sensible. I knew the adjectives enough to apply them to participles and work things out from there. It is easy now to write this though I cannot remember the exact process, only the sense of enlightenment. It would have been less successful if we had not in our minds firmly welded the declensions as well, but the combination worked. I think above all the benefit came from the organised construction of the language, the predictability once you knew the particulars, the essential structure.

It all seemed reasonably promising for the public exams. Indeed, some of us were put in early for the subjects we were good at. I have no idea why I was put in for Maths early. Again, I could learn formulae and could work out sometimes which numbers to substitute for x and y but I failed repeatedly. Science was hopeless. To begin with they put me into Chemistry and Physics as individual subjects. Chemistry was far beyond anything I could manage, largely because it was based on algebraic equations and algebra was beyond my grasp. Geometry and trigonometry came easily enough because you could see what it was all about – physical shapes – and gave enough marks, after three attempts, to counterbalance algebraic ignorance. Yet I can still recite 'x= minus c, plus or minus the square root of b squared over 4ac, all over 2a.' Is this right? As for Science, they put me into a class designed for the hopeless, General Science, which anyone could pass; but I did not, just about reaching Grade 9, the lowest possible.

Those of us who had taken French early were put into a class which was supposed to bridge the gap between O and A-level. I remember nothing of those classes, only that they had no appeal whatsoever. We must have been reading some literature, real French, but it was neither interesting nor possible.

Ultimately, I could only cope with success and saw some subjects as far beyond me.

Options and public exams

Failure through idleness and complacency became a habit, a reality, to me at school. In the 1960s I studied for what were then called O-levels – ordinary levels – in preparation for A-levels, the advanced ones. O-levels were replaced many years later by GCSE's – if you were reasonably capable you did GCE's, if less academic you took CSE's. These were amalgamated later into GCSE, to make everyone feel they were doing the same exam and not imagine that they were a bit thick. This process was undermined by putting people into exams which were higher level or lower, in the latter of which you could reach only a grade C.

You took a bundle of subjects, some of them more or less compulsory, like English and Maths, then a selection from the others on offer. One of the choices I had was to decide between Greek and German. The German teacher, a perfumed Egyptian was introducing the subject for the first time. He thought I would be a good bet for German because I found French easy enough but can never forget the excitement in Mr Mogford's French class when I was asked to recite the present subjunctive of 'porter' and failed:

'Je porte, Tu portes, Il porte, Nous portions' and so on. I knew it was right.

A hushed silence. A pause.

'Again.'

Hesitantly I did it again.

More silence as the class, who knew what was going on, enjoyed seeing one of the good ones struggling on the point of a pin.

'One more chance.'

A third time, the same, each person correctly, I knew. What was going on?

'Four of the strap, Holbourn! *QUE* je porte, *QUE* tu portes and so on.'

But this was silly, I thought. You wanted the verb, not the introductory word. After all, in Latin you wouldn't recite the subjunctives with '*ut*' in front of them, would you? But I kept quiet and did what was needed. Yet I have never lost the sense of injustice and resentment from that day. Indeed, he was wrong. All you needed to do was tell the boys that before reciting the table they must always remember that QUE came before the subjunctive. I have since learnt that the French don't use it much anyway – but that may be the same sort of slovenliness that we see in poorly spoken English now as well.

It was partly for this reason that I turned down Mr Rizkalla's blandishments to join the new Saturday morning German O-level class. I went along a few times during a lovely summer term while a dozen of us sat on chairs around the cricket square.

The German teacher reassured me that I would be able to converse in foreign countries, buy bananas with no difficulty, travel abroad with confidence – all sensible and worthwhile skills.

I went to the Greek teacher, Mr Dunworth. 'Why do you think I should take Greek?' I asked him, not in a challenging way but inquisitively – not that I cared much anyway – I just didn't want to take German, which I was sure would be easy enough to learn later on; after all, they were still speaking it now, whereas Ancient Greek had long gone. It went with Latin of course, which was also coming on reasonably well by then after an awful start two years before.

He looked at me, then looked away. He looked out of the window, studied his fingernails, looked at the door, the floor, anything to avoid, apparently, answering the question. Then at last he produced the truth. 'Er…I don't know really,' he replied.

Both he and his colleague had been Oxbridge Classics graduates who imagined that we, like other years before us and doubtless after as well, would be able to emulate their academic achievements.

I struggled with Greek and Latin for the next two years but passed them both, along with the other subjects which I could cope with. It must have been very disappointing to my father, an engineer, that I was so incapable of going anywhere in science.

When A-level choices came round, it was the same story. I had failed anything that didn't come readily to me – Geography, History, General Science – and passed English language, English Literature, Latin, Greek, French and, at last, grudgingly and at the third attempt, Maths. Why was History so hard for me? Everyone was baffled. I took it twice, on both occasions managing no more than a grade 9 – the lowest possible. I remember there was a green book which was full of material on the unification of Italy, and the second time I learned all about it, so much so that I felt confident – but it came to nothing. Indeed, I even supposed that there might have been a mistake in the marking but there was no challenge.

The choice was straightforward, so I embarked on Latin, Greek and English Literature. We were not, that year, allowed to take Ancient History with the other two classical subjects, a decision enforced by the Head of English, whom I did not like at all. I failed to get an A in some English exam once and I remember him coming to class the day after the results were announced.

He dealt with the obvious successes, then turned to me and, with his weak, pained little smile, he said, 'Well, what happened to you, Holbourn?'

'I don't know, Sir ...' I stuttered.

English went well enough however, though at this, as in everything else, I was idle and every Sunday night was to be found furiously and desperately trying to put together a long essay on D.H. Lawrence or Shakespeare – that is, when I was not struggling over Greek. I can't remember who else we studied. The writing itself was good enough, because I had always taken pride in assembling well-structured sentences, especially because my mother set such high standards. What was I reading? English poetry had leapt off my father's shelves one day. In an empty moment I picked a volume of Keats out and began to read it. What a staggering revelation! Why had no-one told me about it before? His exquisite mastery of language and expression, the tingling he brought to my heart and mind, were beyond any previous experience – and he still does it, half a century later. Yes, of course! It was indeed Keats and maybe Tennyson, an unmemorable poet, who made up the rest of the course. And T.S. Eliot's 'The Waste Land', a poem which lives in my mind and thinking still. After all, as he points out, there is no point in reflecting on things that could have happened if life had been different:

'What might have been is an abstraction
Remaining a perpetual possibility
Only in a world of speculation.'

Regularly, I feel obliged to quote this to people of many different ages as they say 'Oh, if only I'd worked harder' or 'If I'd married George instead of Martin', or 'How did I come to be an accountant? If I'd had the opportunity to go into teaching...' Forget about it: you start from where you are, not from where you might have been.

Translating Latin and Greek into English wasn't too bad but we also had to undertake something called Prose Composition. This was not what it sounded but simply a long passage of English to be turned into the other languages. Time and again, Mr Dunworth would hand back my work – and that of others – with the despairing cry of, 'But it's just not Greek!'

This was utterly depressing, since I would have spent up to six hours over the weekend – usually Sunday night – furiously looking up everything in vocabularies and grammars to get it right. There were one or two of us in the class who had some idea of what they should do, but two of us in particular just didn't get it and had to shrug in despair. Having learnt the skill of failing, we both became reasonably good Classics teachers in the end, for we understood exactly what it felt like to misunderstand and struggle. The cause of my failure to get beyond E at A-level was partly laziness and disinterest, partly wasting lots of time doing nothing. I can remember going out on a Saturday night to a party for more than twenty successive weeks in the Upper Sixth and thinking afterwards that if I had done as much work that year as I had in the previous one, all would have gone swimmingly. It might have been thirty weekends so wasted. so that my weekends became a failure if they did not match that pattern. It was not that I enjoyed parties, or the company; on the contrary, I was embarrassed, had no conversation and stood by a wall in the hope that no-one would approach me. I don't know what it was at all. Such events filled the time I would have failed to use otherwise and made me feel that I was making some sort of development, some kind of social progress; but it was not so.

In reality the best times – and they were dull – were in the Jolly Farmer in Purley or, less successfully, The Windmill in Wallington, just drinking beer with friends, and one in particular whom I still meet for a pint or two.

The reader may wonder what my parents had to say about all this. My father had by this time left home and was living in the north of England and my mother was, I guess, in some sort of dismay, despair and disappointment at the way at least one of her children was coping. How things would have been if my father had been around, is impossible to say.

Education after school ...continued

I failed. What next? You could apply anywhere, with any grades, and I did. There was a book which told you what grades might be acceptable for the course you wanted, and I wanted to carry on learning Greek and Latin. Yet clearly there were no criteria that a respectable university could apply which would excuse my abysmal performance at exams. D in English, E in Latin – I must have known something – and U in Greek, where there was no evidence of anything but total ignorance. It was not the fault of the teachers and I really did know quite a lot of the grammar; I can still recite the aorist middle of assorted Greek verbs, in every conjugation, even now, and Latin was easy by comparison.

Smoking

Applications went in. I tried for Keele, a newish university, and was called for interview. They were unimpressed. I had another interview the next day in Hull, across the Pennines, and hitched a lift in the freezing cold snow. I used to smoke then, just following other people and to avoid seeming socially inept, little roll-ups of Old Holborn or Golden Virginia in liquorice papers, which my mother called 'coffin-nails'. I thought that she meant that they resembled nails but her point was that they led directly to death. I didn't smoke a lot, but as punctuation marks during the day, moments of change, sitting in a room, standing at a bus stop. I can remember sitting in just such a stop on the Pennines on the way to Hull, going through the rituals of the pouch, the papers and the matches, then smoking – the final part of the ritual. I still have the leather tobacco pouch. However, this led to a momentous decision.

One morning at about that time I woke up on a Monday morning unable to breathe. I had smoked for perhaps two years and a half. The decision was simple and I fixed upon the plan: five that day, four the next, three, two one, zero – and it worked. The only time I smoked after that was when I was feeling very lonely when travelling in Egypt and bought a packet of Egyptian cigarettes – then threw them into the Nile after smoking a couple.

Hull University

Returning to education, the professor of Classics in Hull was Professor Norman, a nice Yorkshireman who spoke frankly. 'You haven't done much, have you,' he said. 'Not a lot of evidence to justify our taking you on. Still, I suppose we could take you as a sort of mascot.'

I did not ask what he meant and never found out. Still, there I was, with an identity at last.

The first term I spent in lodgings at 278 Victoria Avenue, Hull, Mr and Mrs Lister. They were kind and tolerant, though Mr Lister was an old curmudgeon. His wife had obviously had students before and was accustomed to their wayward lives, though I think that the university usually sent them people who looked as though they would fit in.

When I left them at the end of the first term to move into university accommodation, Mrs Lister, a kind lady, said 'Well, it was Mr Lister, wasn't it, who made it difficult. He was the bear in the caviar …' – that is exactly what she said, mixing a couple of metaphors which I still have not worked out. Probably, Mr Lister was constantly and justly irritated by my breaking his curfew.

They found me a place in a Hall of Residence. It was bleak. I never settled there, nor at the lectures. I used to go for long walks at night round the city and beyond. One night I walked to Beverly, about eight miles away, for no particular reason. There was the tall spire of the Minster soaring up into the dark night. I have since heard that the friends you make at university are the ones you keep all your life, but this was certainly not so for me, since I made no friends at all.

There were some good lecturers and one or two feeble ones but there was not enough in my head to make much use of it. One of them attempted to teach us a poet called Statius, a silver age poet (1st century AD), very difficult. It was reasonable for him to suppose that people with A-level Latin would cope well enough, but I found it impossible and uninteresting. Later experience proved that to be true but it was not my business to voice a view at that time since I had no authority to speak.

They did not allow me to follow the Greek course – I had failed, after all – but this was a disappointment and did not help. Of course, it would have been useless and I would have felt inadequate in the company of people who knew what they were doing but even so it just felt undermining. What a mess! Then in the January exams I sat gloomily at an exam paper, unable to make anything of the texts before me.

At that moment a revelation enfolded me and I took the first sensible decision in my life, one based on reality rather than pretence. 'I don't know anything,' I thought, 'And I am wasting everyone's time here.'

Standing up, with not a word to anyone or a backward glance, I left the exam hall, strode off to my room, bundled up some possessions and walked away.

It was a cold January day, snowing. To get to the south of England you had either to go west and round the Humber estuary or cross the Humber itself. Since the river was new to me, I took the ferry across and walked for a few days down through Lincolnshire, I know not where, arriving home one afternoon. My mother greeted me frostily.

'What are you doing here?', she asked.

'I've left.'

St Lawrence's Hospital

The subsequent conversation did little justice to either of us and I had to make some sort of life. What was it? Ah yes! I found a job in the kitchens of a local mental hospital as the assistant to the chief kitchen porter, an idle, cheerful   Irishman who took a few days off every week, leaving me to operate huge, clanking machines alone, immersed in steam, and see to it that the thousands of aluminium trays, plates, dishes and so on emerged more or less clean. He would always return with a vast, smiling apology when he had done nothing for two days in my occasional absence. I was conscientious, imagining that the whole place would collapse if they didn't have clean things to use. It was good, too, working with one of the inmates, a man who was deemed to be a higher grade than many and fit, so to speak, for human company. His name was not quite Old Scratch-Arse, but something like it which I can't remember.

'You don't want to go into vat wing at the end,' he told me one day in his gruff voice, consonants unclear until you got used to him.

'Why not?'

'They're the low-grades. Can't do anyfink wiv'em. Never see the light of day.' What luckless parents, what dismal lives were concealed within these pictures!

Six months or more I was there, keeping a sort of respectability and putting some money away; and it was very good to be in a version of the real world with people who had not gone to school much.

Altrincham and Barbara

Where did my visit to my father in Cheshire happen? I cannot put it in place but it was a very strong experience. I think it must have been immediately after Hull. He had left home and was now living in Altrincham, working for I know not whom. I think he would not be able to deny that he was a serial philanderer, and I can see why he was successful in this. He had an eager, boyish smile and an air of vulnerability, as well as the ability to talk on many subjects.

He allowed me to stay since I had nowhere else. He was living with a lady, a bright, sensible, equally charming, northern woman, who would say, 'There's nothing better than cleanliness.' I thought long and hard about this claim, deciding that she was definitely wrong. Generosity? Kindness? She was still married to a salesman of accelerated freeze-dried coffee. I met him once, as well as their two daughters, an uninspiring man who evidently did not see his inadequacies. He was probably decent enough but he was not up to Barbara's level of independent thought.

Dad's relationship with Barbara was utterly true, entirely straight, quietly humorous and they teased each other happily. It makes me reflect that the people you marry are not necessarily the right people, only the ones you happen to meet at the right time. I know this from my own experience as well.

Rather than sponge off my father I managed to get a job at Manchester airport, in the department which dealt with loading meals and alcohol onto the aircraft. All I had to do was make sure there were enough plastic knives and forks on each flight – thousands of them. For this I was paid £11 a week, a very low wage even then.

To get there I had to catch a bus at 5.30 in the morning and return at 10.30 at night, by which time the buses had stopped and I had to walk. Since this meant getting home in time for four hours sleep, I decided to leave after a few months but not before asking for a rise. They turned me down flat and I walked out.

Return to Purley

Yes, it was after this that I went back to Purley, a road which my father called Cold Stodge Lane – Old Lodge Lane. Earlier, when I was studying Virgil at A-level, I used to walk up the road at night towards Kenley aerodrome and the Wattenden Arms a couple of miles away. There was a bend and dip in the road half a mile into the darkness, a chill and fright I can remember now. But the moon! It echoed a passage from the sixth book of the Aeneid, where Aeneas is visiting the underworld to see his dead father's ghost and find out his mission. There in the gloom gleamed out the ghost of Dido, his abandoned lover who had killed herself when he left her to found Rome. It was an impossible choice but he had to do it. How do you choose between love and duty? This has been a challenge all my life and my heart was with him, and remains so. Human life is based upon tension, like a tight-rope. You have to watch, balance, keep your eyes fixed or even closed, with at one end duty, the right thing to do, propriety, and at the other whim, desire, longing, wishes and wants. They tug against each other and you stand there, sometimes shuffling one way, sometimes inching back, all the time wobbling and never really learning – except to survive, since there is no safety net – or there wasn't for me, other than to shrug, leap off and see where I landed.

Anyway, there was Dido's wraith amidst the shadows. He saw her like one who:

aut videt, aut vidisse putat per nubila lunam.

'-sees, or thinks he has seen, the moon through the clouds'.

And there were the clouds and the moon between them! I think it was that experience that tied me to Virgil and therefore Latin poetry, which I continue to read even now.

One of the best things I had learnt from my father in Altrincham, was a practical approach to daily life. For example, at that time I was very careless about formality, in an adolescent way. We would prepare our meals and he said to me one day:

'Shall I lay the table?'

'I don't usually.' I didn't, ever.

'Why not?'

'Can't be bothered.'

I am ashamed to see this written down and have been ashamed of this casual, idle, throw-away remark ever since, issued as though I knew that his fussiness was worthless and merely conventional.

'Hmm…well, one of the things I have learnt since living on my own is to *be* bothered,' he observed.

And so, it has been for me ever since that moment: I have taken care to do things better for the most part.

There is so much I have missed out up to this point – the Catholic church and my relationship with it, my sister, my brother, my other sister, my failures as a cricketer, cycling, walking, my dislike of cars, travel sickness, the relationship between my parents… all are worthy of individual chapters.

Mum

I don't think that either my sister or I got on particularly well with our mother. She was an intelligent woman, five years older than Dad, but quite sharp and difficult; certainly not affectionate. They had met in Ceylon – now Sri Lanka – and married there when he was 21. They presumably thought that they were well matched but they were not, in our experience. One of the weekly events which we watched playing out was the Sunday drama when Dad would ask Mum whether and where she would like us all to go out for a drive in the afternoon. This led to interminable discussions and furious rages, though I cannot remember the stances of either of them clearly. I am sure that Dad wanted to do something along the family line and that Mum did not want to comply, using domestic chores as an excuse – but that sounds a more conventional account than probably occurred. My sister and I used to listen to these battles from the next room. We knew the script, the postures, even the outcome, and derived some sort of amusement from the predictability of it all. At the same time, we both felt that Dad was the victim in the process.

One of the eternals and still unresolved mysteries was the religious stance of our mother. Shelagh and I occasionally asked her whether she had become a Catholic but she was cagy about it, so we assumed that they had a mixed marriage. She was entirely supportive of Dad in his aspirations for us but she herself remained outside the fold, so to speak.

Mum was a very strong influence on our education. When I was six, she came and looked over my shoulder as I was doing some homework. I could sense that something had gone wrong.

'How do you spell 'summer?' she asked sharply.

'S-U-M-M-E-R', I replied.

'Then why have you spelt it *S-U-M-E-R*?' she scornfully inquired.

I was deeply ashamed. Mum was never the sort of

person to say 'Never mind, don't do it again, it'll be all right next time,' or anything like that. In saying this I am in no way criticising her approach, for it worked and I am not sure that a more relaxed manner would have had the same effect, for I could only respect her standards. After all, I was not the sort of person who made spelling mistakes and there is no doubt that that occasion made me a scrupulously careful speller of words ever since. I am open to challenge, of course…

<u>Shelagh</u>

My sister Shelagh and I have always been good friends. This relationship really cemented itself when we were growing up and our parents were finding things difficult so that we were amused witnesses to it all, not appreciating the misery, bitterness and suffering Mum and Dad were inflicting on each other in their different ways.

However, apart from that we just used to spend a lot of time together. We both remember some of the walks we undertook, unbelievable now. On one occasion we undertook a walk up to and along a wooded hill not far away called Riddlesdown. If our parents knew or minded, I cannot remember but we had a good time, just walking during a hot day and chatting.

More ambitious still was when we decided to walk along the Brighton Road – from Old Lodge Lane – towards Brighton. I cannot remember how far we got but it was certainly as far as Gatwick Airport.

How did we get back? I have no idea. It was a very hot summer's day and I remember that Shelagh's arms were reddened with the sun.

We still get on very well as good friends with mutual understanding though living fifty miles from each other. Probably it is because we grew up together as common victims and observers of our parents.

Shelagh has had some interesting and colourful relationships. On one occasion, whose details I may have misremembered, she asked me if I would go and stay with her in her flat in Crystal Palace, because her husband, John Edmonds, had left her and she could not pay the rent by herself. Of course, I agreed but things developed in a different way. I liked John. If you know the Belloc poem:

'Behold you now the Nordic man
And be as like him as you can.
His legs are long, his mind is slow,
His hair is lank and full of tow.'

John's mind was not slow but he resembled the picture in that book to a T.

Then an odd occurrence took place. Shelagh moved away to live with John's best friend Eric, a nice, balanced man whom I never knew well, so that I was left in the flat – until John moved back. There I found myself, incredibly, living with my brother-in-law, another unplanned novelty. The most dramatic day came when I had prepared a meal for myself and left it on the side in the kitchen. I left the room to lay the table; there was an almighty crash from the kitchen. I returned to find that the wall cabinets, with their glass doors, had fallen off the walls. There on the floor were cups, plates, a meal, cupboards, all in a mess. I walked away, unable to devise any solution. It was a crucial occasion. I returned to the kitchen and picked up a cup, then a plate, then everything, one by one. It took time, of course, but there was no other way.

From this disaster I learnt that when faced with a catastrophe you do not panic, or blame, or shout, or cry: you just do something to sort it out. This has been priceless in subsequent life and I recommend the whole process to any reader: just get on with it.

Religious questions

Every week Dad during our childhood would take Shelagh and me to Mass at the big church in Gravesend, St John's, with Fr Mundy. Sometimes when we were late, we would hurtle off to a smaller, nearer church called St Mary's. It was so obvious that this was what you did, attending Mass, that there was never any question.

At John Fisher there was always Benediction on Fridays, for fifteen minutes after school, and I always attended, though slightly troubled that the purpose was not in tune with my religious sense. I was in some turmoil about the church. On the one hand there was the undermining, cheap and conventional thought that if you've been to one Mass, you've been to them all, so you didn't need to keep going and it would be better to cut the shackles and get on with life in freedom. On the other – though there were a few other confusing thoughts – there was the fairly firm conviction that there was nowhere else to go and that it was part of my life. I could not become an Anglican or anything else, and knew, without expressing it verbally, that I was never going to throw it all away, never going to be nothing.

Much of this had come from reading, especially Ronald Knox, who had been through the same qualms and difficulties himself. Later on, I read Newman's *'Apologia pro vita sua'*, a difficult book but another in which an intelligent man (like Knox, I mean) explained the difficulty and rationale of his trials in dealing with the church.

I had a sympathy with Newman, irrational because I knew his name from the House system at John Fisher. There were six 'houses' and you were allotted to one of them when you arrived.

'You're in Newman', said some teacher when allocating us. Newman were useless, usually coming last, whereas More (dark blue), Becket (red), Challoner (green) were successful in most sports. Who were yellow and orange? Newman wore light blue, a colour with little impact. Ah yes! One of them was Bede. Not until much later in life di I come to know why these men were famous.

There was much intellectual argument within my own head over religious truth and I concluded that, although I didn't like it, that was where I belonged. This has remained true since then: I don't like the Church and care very little for the liturgy, the priests, the congregation; yet I go to Mass every Sunday because it is the right thing to do, regardless of my tastes. Undoubtedly, I had major problems when the English liturgy became the usual practice: I couldn't, and cannot, bear the awful translations of the Latin, though they have improved a little under scrutiny in the last few years. Even so I am not reliant on having a Latin Mass to ensure my presence. Either it is true or it isn't; it isn't a matter of my preference. Here in Hertford, there is a Latin Mass, Tridentine, every month and I went once. The distinction between the Tridentine rite and a Latin Mass is not to be dealt with in this narrative, though it would be important to understand the difference. Anyway, that Tridentine Mass was useless for me, but that is a major chapter which I have no time to develop here. I will say only this: regardless of my taste and enjoyment I will not miss Mass without due cause – and I am not looking for one.

It is true that I lost track of Catholic practice for about three years; however, when I arrived in South Africa, one of the first things I did was to find the nearest Catholic Church. This was not for social reasons or to find people of like mind but because I knew that this was what I had to do.

But we have not embarked on our journey yet and much of the above is speculative rather than narrative.

Dad and Africa

My year in Africa came about because, as well as the money I had saved up from washing-up at St Lawrence's Hospital, I had inherited £300 from the last testament of Great Uncle Will, whom I had never met. It seemed a good idea to go and visit my father in South Africa, where he had fled in company with Barbara from Manchester. A romantic by nature, he had met her there when working for a few months. Dad had had a series of affairs, doubtless in search of something he had not yet found. In Barbara he found his treasure.

He was at that time a salesman of level-measuring equipment. Having worked for a firm called Powers-Samas he moved on to learn more about electronics and how they could be applied practically. He had little formal education and left school, apparently literate and civilised, I think at the age of 16. The particular skill he had developed was installing equipment which measured the level of materials in vats. For example, a vat of sugar is filled through a series of tubes and pipes and would continue to do so until the end of the world unless some trigger made the mechanism stop. Dad partly devised and certainly sold a contraption which did this. He showed me one once. To an imaginative mind it resembled a protruding member of the male anatomy extending horizontally from the side of a vat into which it was screwed. Inside it had electronic sensors which prompted other machinery to stop pouring the sugar as soon as it reached the level of the extension. Clearly this was very useful in a country which relied on sugar production, like South Africa, and did away, I suppose, with the need for people standing at the side and yelling 'O.K, Switch off now!'.

He was, in the general view, a charmer. Certainly, a very nice bloke, and we got on well, though had intellectual and political differences. He was, he said, a Liberal, though I did not really know what that meant politically except that he did not see himself as part of any establishment party. And why, I wonder now, was there a big book on his shelves called 'My Struggle'? This was 'Mein Kampf', Hitler's explanation of how he had made up his mind. Dad was not a fascist or even much of a Conservative, and he had probably acquired it to help him understand how the Second World War had occurred. Where was I, politically? Probably where I am now, essentially sceptical of the system and longing for a benign and wise dictatorship.

White charger

I had absorbed or inherited some of Dad's idealism and had decided that, since I now had a bit of money, I would go to Durban and persuade him to return to his wife, my mother. What a fool I was, imagining I was a knight on a white horse galloping away to right a wrong, imagining that I knew how mature and experienced people thought and operated. Of course, at the time it seemed straightforward and simple; it took more experience to get inside the minds and hearts of those involved. However, my task now is to recall a range of pictures and impressions which would be better unpacked.

Travels: to Athens

I had not travelled much before, just hitch-hiked round Europe for a couple of summers in the last two years of school with my friend Mick – not really a friend but one who was cleverer than me and could get away with doing no work, unless secretly, for his Latin and Greek A-levels, whereas I did nothing and paid the price. My grades, following my worthless sixth form, were D, U and E, as were due to me, having done no work at all. The D was in English. In one of those two years three of us, including Robert McGrath, went and hitch-hiked here and there round Europe and, despite there being three of us, we regularly were offered lifts. In retrospect this seems beyond belief but it happened.

Having money and time – I had already left Hull University, as I explained above, because I was getting nowhere – it seemed a good idea to charge off to South Africa on the mission described. Not for me, however, the boredom of air travel, though I had never flown. I knew that Africa was a big continent and that it would be simple to take an air flight to get there; to do so, however, would mean skipping over vast tracts of humanity as though they did not exist. For a long time, I had hated the notion of airliners, huge metal tubes squirted through the air with no regard for anything but making money – an outcome which depended on their maintaining the lives of their cargo. It just seemed an interesting idea to travel over as much land as possible, to make as much of the opportunity as I could.

The plan was to hitch to Athens, take a boat across to Alexandria and see what happened thenceforward. But we have still not embarked on our journey yet and the above paragraph is speculative rather than narrative.

Sometime in the middle of July it was, 1969. I was 20. How did I get down to Dover? Train? Somebody's car? Probably, thumbing a lift: paying for travel was against the principles around at the time. Then, somewhere in northern France, as I stood with increasing despair at the roadside, a white van pulled up.

'Where are you going?' asked a big, cheerful, ginger-headed face.

'Athens,' I said. 'The map had told me that I could take a boat from there across the Mediterranean to Africa somewhere.'

'OK. I'll take you to Salonika. This is Flipper, by the way. We're dropping him off in Munich.'

Flipper sat in the passenger seat, a thin, lithe lad with not much to say. This large Devonian driver was on his way to deliver the barrel of cider in the back of the van to a friend in Istanbul.

How long was I in the van? Long enough to stay at Flipper's place in Munich overnight, to hear a good deal about Bristol, to remain a passive listener to loud and somewhat boorish conversations. I think there was someone else in the van, as well as the cider, also on his way to Istanbul. I really wanted to go to Istanbul but more than fifty years later have still not done so.

Flipper was a circus acrobat. Nothing else remains in my mind about him.

In Salonika I went to the railway station and bought a ticket for Athens, then somehow reached Piraeus, the port, and took the two-day trip across to Alexandria. But no! While I was in Athens I found somewhere to stay overnight, a room right next to an outdoor cinema screen, just beside the Acropolis. Not much sleep, of course, with the Greek soundtrack booming and incomprehensible lights flickering. Also, while there I visited the Acropolis and the Parthenon as well. I didn't understand it at all, having studied only the language at school, and that 2,500 years old. One of the delights, however, was looking at the signs and being able to work out what they must mean. I remember looking at my railway ticket and seeing on it '*σιδηροδρομο*s' (*siderodromos*). What fun it was to see that I was travelling on the *iron drome*, the iron road.

Athens to Africa

Presumably I took a boat across the Mediterranean, landing, I remember, in Alexandria. This was amazing because as soon as you disembarked you could smell spices, nothing but spices, such as you would never experience in Europe. This was Africa! Another world, a world beyond Europe.

No other memories come to me of Alexandria except narrow streets; nor is it clear how I reached Cairo – it must have been on a train. There must have been a ticket office in Cairo and a means to find it but the pictures are all gone.

The journey from Cairo down through the Sahara was memorable. On the boat I was travelling in the lowest class – third, I think. Three boats were being pulled along by a large tug, side by side. There were huge earthenware water-jugs, as tall as a man, standing on the decks, always full, so that at least we were constantly refreshed from the searing heat. After a few hours' travelling I decided to move across into the second-class boat, just to look, and it was there that I discovered an unpleasant truth: the reason for the jugs being full was simply that men were dipping great buckets into the water and pouring it into the jugs, so we were drinking Nile water all the time. I became very ill with a vile stomach upset.

At some point on the edge of the desert I was approached by a man leading three camels. He wanted to sell me a ride on one and I agreed. It lasted no more than five minutes and was one of the most uncomfortable rides you could devise. You had to hold on to the saddle pommel because you were swaying sideways all the time, peering nervously down at the great, curved neck.

There was a train: I can visualise a huge, silver locomotive in the vast, open, sandy desert. What an enormous place a desert is! I can understand why people are drawn to it and the attraction of simply walking off, mile after mile, into the wilderness was strong. My fourth-class ticket meant that I had not paid for a seat, only a place on the train, though did not realise it. The experienced travellers knew exactly what to do. They pushed straight onto the train with their bags, children and bundles and took up their places on the wooden benches. Since I was a polite and ignorant Englishman I waited until they were aboard, then found a scrap of floor, with my bundle of sleeping bag containing everything.

There were two major issues. The first was ventilation. There was no glass, only wooden slats. If they were opened, the Nubian desert blasted into the carriage, making it impossible to breathe anything but sand; if the slats were closed the temperature became unbearable. Since I was on the floor, leaning against my rucksack, I was not involved in the decisions, only the suffering of both discomforts.

The other problem was sanitary arrangements. There was a little door and a hole in the floor, beneath which the rails and sand hurtled by. The latter I was obliged to use fairly often because of my gruesome stomach upset, caused by drinking some of the Nile on the long lake from Sudan. The best part of that boat journey was being looked after by a group of young lads who tried with genuine concern to cure me of my fever and sickness by smearing me in lemon juice, freshly squeezed from the fruit they were carrying in sacks. The rail journey lasted for 24 hours and sleep must have been an intermittent comfort.

Uganda

We arrived in Kampala, the Ugandan capital and somehow, I found a very cheap room to stay in. Things improved though memory is hazy hereabouts. One night I walked down the road to a bar to see what the beer was like. Some of it was a sort of pinky-grey and had the texture of vegetable soup, as is quite a lot of the beer brewed in Africa, but I found something more palatable.

There were times when the warnings of an Australian I had met on a boat seemed likely to come true.

'You'll be knifed, of course,' he told me.

There were several encounters which demonstrated my idiocy and inexperience, one of which I remember vividly, but it was one which again I survived unscathed.

Southern and central Africa.

There must have been a journey through the country still called Southern Rhodesia then. I remember going through Zambia – Northern Rhodesia – or at least to its border, with loudspeakers everywhere proclaiming 'One Zambia, One Nation' but that might have been on the way back. It is, on reflection, clear that the times were full of change: Northern Rhodesia had become Zambia during the same year and South Africa was changing its racial leanings, as we shall see.

Salisbury I am just recalling, with those glorious purple jacaranda trees in bloom all along the roads in the city. Bulawayo came into it somewhere; perhaps I went by train through the country. Bulawayo was known as 'a railway city' but it has all escaped me. Yes! I do remember thinking then that the country had an air of civilisation and order, culture and calm, much as Kenya presumably had twenty years before, as I had heard from people who lived there. It was a beautiful country, utterly African with an overlay of England. There was glorious, vast farmland everywhere.

Then there was Swaziland. The mention of its name brings it back to me, a lovely, green, mountainous country. Somehow, I was walking over a mountain road, down through piney woods towards...Mbabane, was it? Names unearth themselves, probably wrongly.

South Africa

At last, I was on the borders of South Africa, more or less penniless. The sensible and officious border guards asked some pertinent questions. Why was I there? Where was I going? Where was I proposing to live? And how? Obviously, they didn't want some vagrant to come along and be a burden to the state.

I told them that I was going to stay with my father in Durban and somehow managed to find his address in my luggage. They were very decent about it and let me in – I wouldn't have blamed them if they had turned me away, though I had no back-up plan.

How did I get to Durban? Probably by train, though how did I pay the fare?

The railway station in Durban was very handsome, a replica, someone told me, of Dublin station.

I stayed with my father in his flat for a few days while finding a room to rent, which was easy enough. I had few belongings, of course, so needed little space. There were a couple of addresses and I have a photograph of one, a ghastly white block with a balcony looking into a central courtyard, a black and white cat peering down. Then there was a room in the house of an oldish lady. Was the suburb called Berea? Something Gardens? It was close to the city centre in an area which reminds me, on reflection, of the better part of Tooting in its atmosphere and age. At all events I had to pay the rent and needed employment.

I should point out that this time was still the time of Apartheid, euphemistically called 'separate development' of blacks and whites, though on the cusp of change. In what follows there are a couple of anecdotes which reflect badly on the Afrikaners but such behaviour was typical of only one kind, the more entrenched Afrikaners. This was the first time I had met genuine racism in a bitterly hostile and frankly subhuman form. Most of the Afrikaners were from farming stock, humane and kind. Probably city life brought out the worst in others, though that is speculation.

Early and desperate sales employment

The first job I almost had was selling the Encyclopaedia Britannica. I learnt a lot from watching this. One evening I went out with a real salesman and we visited a young couple in a flat. The salesman had some extracts from the encyclopaedia, some enormous, colourful maps, charts and pictures, all sorts of powerful images promising enormous wisdom and comprehensive understanding of the world.

The young couple were bemused and overwhelmed by this promise of total knowledge. The salesman was convincing, professional, impressive and persuasive. They bought it, though they were young, recently married and with no obvious wealth. But who needs wealth when you have the tree of knowledge on your shelves to enrich you? For that is exactly the way it seemed: the salesman was the devil, the young couple Adam and Eve. It was horrible to watch and listen as they fell for his wiles, the snake who had wriggled through their doorstep, invited in by unsuspecting innocents. The truth of this became clear after we left and the salesman disclosed his contempt for people who bought the books. It was over for me. Never could I have sold anything on those terms.

Another selling job came my way. The Indian Ocean is infested with cockroaches, about which I learnt enough to realise that they are worth exterminating. You cannot kill them by treading on them: they have too hard a carapace, even though they look like great beetles. They live in the most disgusting places and conditions and naturally carry diseases with them. As a result, there are countless products available to kill them, spray them, dissuade them, all of which are in competition with teach other.

I cannot remember what was special about the product or process I became involved in, only that the firm was called 'Wonder Pest' and I had to knock on door after door to persuade householders to purchase it. It soon became so dull that I would wander hopelessly along the streets, working out ways to enliven things. Might I go to the next door and say:

'Good morning, madam! Are you infested by verminous, filthy creatures? Yes, I can see you are! Never mind! I have here the very thing you have been desperately seeking all your life…'

Or perhaps:

'Good afternoon, Madam. I'm Wonder Pest.'

A few days later there was another opportunity, a job offered by a firm called Unique Designs and Fashions, owned and run by a Dutchman. We undertook our sales in all sorts of venues. I can remember being sent into a tall office block and going into a room where some girls were having their morning tea break. There were industrial sites as well: how many people, I wonder, have been thrown out of an umbrella factory? Somewhere I have a diary from those days, with addresses and times of appointments, reminding me that it was all real rather than a nightmare.

More ambitious were the 'field trips'. All we had to do, as a team of salesmen, was to drive to another town like Ladysmith, then take a map and divide the town into five – the number of the team – and into sections of three, morning, afternoon and evening. You were on your own on the streets.

Another line was:

'Good morning, Madam. I'm from Unique Designs.'

I did this a couple of times but it was only for my amusement and certainly failed to raise even a twisted smile. Of course, there was plenty of time to reflect on the truth of this claim: we are all from unique designs, though along the same pattern, and the differences are astonishing, and crucial. Individuality and its necessity are at the heart of humanity.

Here is a sample of a doorstep interview:

Knock knock.

'Yes?'

'Is the Madam in?'

'I'll fetch her,' the black servant replies.

Along comes some elegant white woman.

'Good morning, madam. Do you by any chance make your own dresses?' I learned very quickly not to ask this question, since a negative would end the conversation. I did not then have the gift of developing a new dialogue, which would have gone:

'You don't? Oh, you're missing a wonderful opportunity to escape from the prison of those goods available in store. I can tell just from looking at you that you have better taste than that – that you have an eye for design. Just look at these colourful fabrics! I can just see you in... no, no! Look here! That tasteful green... imagine it with the necklace you're wearing at the moment...' and so on.

Instead, I opened my book of samples and offered them to examine. It was a fine book, containing all sorts of colours and materials, possibly tempting even to someone who, two minutes before, had been sitting reading – they still did not have television then.

When they had given an order for one, two, as many materials as they liked, I asked them for a 10% deposit. This was absolutely crucial, as you will see. Off I would go to the house next door and continue the patter.

We would all meet in a cafe for lunch – which we paid for by pooling our deposits and totting up our costs – then continue in the afternoon, whose deposits paid for our evening meal, then the evening to collect enough for our hotel for the night.

Such excursions lasted for three days and were genuinely successful. Indeed, I became more than proficient, a more successful doorstep seller than anyone else, even the most experienced. I think the reasons were threefold. In the first place, if you didn't sell, you didn't eat. Secondly, the sense of competition was quite strong and one or two of the 'team' were utterly obnoxious and subhuman; one Afrikaner youth once urged the driver to commit murder:

'Eh, look at that f***ing kaffir! Run him down – it'll be one less…' and he meant it.

The third factor was Englishness, so that the ladies concerned were quietly pleased to have this young, reasonably spoken youth on their doorstep. It was an unsought but priceless asset. In the event I was promoted to be a Field Manager, which meant that I earned not only my proportion of the order but also another proportion of my underlings' sales – 25%, I think.

There was a different sort of experience when we made a field trip out of Natal, down the coast to the beautiful Zululand. It all went well until one morning I knocked on a door and it was answered by the usual African woman.

'May I speak to the Madam?' I asked as usual.

Coolly the reply came to wrongfoot me utterly:

'I am the madam,' she replied, with less hostility than my question deserved.

There was a problem with this job, which I did for a couple of months. You were paid your commission only at the end of the month – but by then, of course, you had spent it on simply living, so there was nothing left. I could not pay the rent. A fine lady in the office, Mrs Porten, an Indian lady of traditional proportions, knowing my plight simply paid me anyway and said she would sort it out – I suppose by cooking the books. It was a wonderful rescue but made me realise that I had to get a different sort of job, one where you turned up, worked, went home and received payment regularly.

To my great delight I found yesterday along with my books one of the orderbooks from those expeditions, from Durban to Pietermarizburg and Johannesburg, through suburbs and industrial areas.

The docks in Durban: fork lifts.

In Durban, there are docks, full of people driving, loading, moving, heaving the goods on and off ships to be transported hither and thither. I was interviewed by one of what the English called '*roinecks*' – red-necks, a thick-necked Afrikaner named J.J. Van Zyl. He gave me a list of do's and don'ts. The third or fourth sternly instructed the driver:

'No riding on the forks.' At the end, again: 'You must not ride on the forks.'

I learnt from these rules the general principle of law: look at a list of laws and you can deduce the sort of crimes likely to be committed.

I had never driven anything before, nor since. It was perfect: we worked 24-hour shifts, which meant we had to be on duty all day and all night, though it was accepted that at night you could hide away and slumber amongst the sacks of grain at the back of a shed somewhere. I did not need lodgings, saving more money.

We were a mixed bunch of drivers. Some of them were men who could get no work anywhere else but didn't mind. They were, as they put it, 'poor whites'. Many of us were odd characters who had just turned up. There was one South African lad, very proud of his country. 'God's own country,' he called it every time. Then there was a well-educated youth who used to enjoy making up English words to classical melodies, a habit I still enjoy now, always remembering the words he devised for Beethoven's third piano concerto, the third movement:

'The way you look at me, anyone would think I was a fool...'

Perhaps he learnt it from somewhere else.

There was a bearded man whom I met again in England, a devotee of a problematic style of education, the Rudolf Steiner schools – actually quite interesting. There were many hours just sitting on the dockside waiting for something to do. It was a simple machine to drive, made by Hyster. There was a steering wheel, a canopy in case it fell over and you would otherwise be crushed, and two pedals. The one on the right was the brake, the other was the accelerator. It was ingenious in that it tipped to left or right according to whether you wanted forward or backward, before you depressed the pedal to move it into action. Sitting there one afternoon there was a yell in front of me:

'Stacker!' This was not an obscenity or insult: we were stacker drivers. It was one of the stevedores, a team of Africans who unloaded the pallets – and that is another story – requiring me to move backward from the ship's side moored in front of me, so that a crane load of materials could be placed on the dockside.

Startled from my empty musings, I put the accelerator down sharply – but the wrong way: the machine instantly sped forward, the forks pointing to the side of the ship. There were yells and shouts as we hurtled forward. What would have happened had I not found the brake in time? Either the forks would have pierced the ship's hull or the Hyster would have plunged deep into the dock with me still aboard, never to be seen again.

Here I am to tell the tale so it must have worked, though there were one or two other hairy moments. One came from a mischievous colleague. I heard a screech of anguish behind me once. I looked back in alarm, to see him standing laughing to think I had been taken in by his pretence at having been run over. How limited were our opportunities for humour.

At the end of a day, we had to park our machines in a shed somewhere. On one occasion I was perched on a very big machine driving back to the shed. The roadway was clear in front of me and there was no-one to be seen. I was filled with thrills and put my foot down, travelling faster than ever before. It was so exciting! But somewhere in the middle of this it dawned on me that I was a danger to anyone else and that such emotions, such excitement were unacceptable. I could never trust myself in a motor vehicle on the road. That is one of the reasons I have never sought to drive.

Another driving problem was eyesight. Initially I had wanted to be a crane driver and applied but was not allowed to because of poor eyesight. Glasses seemed the answer but were not allowed: you might be unsighted for a second by the frames of the glasses and you were therefore a danger to others.

After months of this I had enough to come back to England. It had gradually become clear that this sort of life could be nothing but an interlude and that I really ought to continue with the education I had irresponsibly abandoned.

Back to England

Since I had missed out on the southern part of my journey it seemed a good idea to travel overland to Nairobi, then fly the rest of the way, but it did not work out. I was given a lift: the diary says *'Classy Indian sports car to Joburg. Stayed in YMCA.'*

From here on I shall have to decipher my tiny writing from the diary and either quote it directly or write down the events it recalls.

'Train 12 noon to Pretoria. 4 miles out of Pretoria, Oudetepoorti. Silent young ladies with 3 sons.'

There was a lift from a man who had vast amounts to tell me about the Freemasons, of which he was one. His mantra, his key phrase, was 'Let's face it…', by which he meant 'What I'm telling you is true, whether you like it or not.' He took me to Warmbad, from which I was taken in the back of a pickup truck to Nylstroom, a bland town. There was a notice at the roadside:

'Department of Water Affairs. Boring Station.'

A man in a big green car driving from Port Elizabeth stopped and took me to Potgietersrus. It was disappointingly clear that I was not going to reach Botswana – formerly Bechuanaland – which had sounded very interesting, since it was on the cusp of change, as were so many countries thereabouts.

'To Pietersburg with Mercenary Medicine Man'.

A lady from Bulawayo stopped and we paused somewhere for coffee. Some while and a few miles later we saw monkeys waiting for scraps.

'Haha, we haven't left much,' she said.

Then a bit further, I told her that in fact we had: my bag, with money, passport, vaccination forms and camera. We drove back – and they were still there at the roadside. It was very hot.

We reached the border at Louis Trichardt, where I was obliged to hand over 300 dollars – I don't know why, whether I got it back or what it was for. Probably some sort of security, which I would get back on leaving the country. We entered Bulawayo, a clean, relaxed town full of big, long streets and large white buildings, very quiet. I think the lady left me somewhere there in town.

From there I found myself on the way to Victoria Falls. A man from Warwick, a retired engineer turned cattle farmer, took me five miles, a sawmill manager with many stories, a tin-mine owner and a railway worker. Then came the man building a hotel at Victoria Falls, 270 miles away. We made the journey in three hours and I have never felt so close to imminent death as I did then. He was very calm and easy-going and there was little traffic. He said that I could stay in one of the huts his workers were using on the site.

I remember beer and the sounds of scamperings in the bushes near the hut.

Since then, stories have abounded in news bulletins of people being slithered off African river banks by crocodiles awaiting their daily feast. It never occurred to me at the time that there might be any danger and I can remember nothing threatening.

I was there for perhaps 48 hours – two nights, anyway. There were fronds, palms, scrubby plants everywhere and a notice saying 'Beware Crocodiles.' And there were the falls, the mightiest and most powerful natural phenomenon I had ever seen.

'Rashly buy air ticket to Kariba.' There was a vast dam there.

I couldn't eat for a day and a half and spent the time just doing nothing and looking. Most people who stay there for more than a day or so spend their time in a bar – and I can't blame them.

I discovered the wonders of John Collins – the cocktail – after a long walk along the gorges. I loafed about awaiting the aeroplane. It came, we flew, I was not sick and we landed at Kariba. Somehow, I got to the town, eleven miles away, and stayed in a cheap hotel.

The next day (October 1st) an air hostess took me to the main road, then a bank clerk to Kaori, where there was a tsetse fly control squirting stop. A man in a van stopped.

'Are you going to Salisbury?'

'Yes!'

'Want to fly?'

'Er ... yes!'

We drove through tobacco farms to an airstrip, where we climbed into his little monoplane and we landed just outside Salisbury.

The days are full of words and incidents:

'Old colonial German couple to Riverside...Hairy Irish hitch-hikers... couple from Sevenoaks KS on Holiday at Umali...'

'Bank closed – no money. 'Portugal holiday today': Of course. Cats in dustbins...pavement cafes...walk five miles to lighthouse...prawn omelette...rusty old ship on white beach...horrid swampy place...station – thousands of people...idle day waiting for jacket to be cleaned...'

Immense confusion over money and ticket at border, never mind the details.   They phoned Blantyre   for   instructions   over what to do with me, since I had no ticket, had to leave, could get no Malawi money and could therefore not buy a ticket.

I was put in the guard's van, which was then detached   from the train and left in a siding, pushed there by a huge diesel.

'We are looking for one wire to connect you to the

train again.'

At last, they found one and we travelled at a fast-walking pace to the border.

'Lift with missionary to Blantyre.'

Sat 9th: BHC (British High Commission) closed until Monday: have to stay the weekend.

Mon 11th: Zambian consul not available until p.m. Traipse about, v irritable with sham officialdom. Resigned to staying another night.

'Long talk with apparent windbag who turns out to have far more sense than I have'.

Thur 14th: Up early to climb mountain path, initially with two guides.

Then I went on and had to rest every hundred yards in the lizard-infested pine forests. Shaded but very hot indeed. I was fascinated by the lines of ants crossing the winding path. Each ant was nearly an inch long and they followed each other in military formation. I had decided to go to Chilwe's Hole and Williams Falls but never found them. The rain fell as I reached a forest village, then an ancient land-rover carried me back to Zomba, then another lift to Blantyre, where I was given a very good Spanish omelette.

From there I seem to have gone straight to Mombasa, the first international city I had been in since Johannesburg. I had three lifts there, the first 3 miles, the second thirty, the third 270. Within ten

minutes I had been offered opium, sex and black-market money. The room I hired was only a bed – and that for just six hours, since it was not a hotel but a brothel.
I walked down to the sea which was lined with huge baobab trees, then back to the town and into a couple of bars.

In one of them a small girl began winking at me, then moved closer.

'My name is Doris,' she said. 'I love you.'

I was nonplussed and baffled, not knowing how to respond, other than with amiable gratitude.

Then she said, 'Shall we go somewhere else?'

Innocently, I agreed and we left to go to the next bar.

'Are you going to buy me a drink?' she asked winningly.

'Sorry, I haven't got any money,' I told her.

'WHAT? You bring a girl into a bar and you can't even buy her a drink?' She called on the support of the large bartender, who looked capable of anything; it seemed the time for me to retreat.

On the way back it seemed interesting to pass through Mozambique. One of the stacker drivers said that he used to go home regularly to Portugal.

'Portugal? But that's in Europe. Surely you can't

afford it all the time.'

'No, Portugal, just along the coast.' He meant Mozambique, a colony of Portugal.

I remember little of the country but do remember seeing, on a wide, white sandy beach miles long, a wrecked ship, all black and rusty orange, evidently abandoned there years ago. The background of such a mournful sight was the dazzling blue of the Indian Ocean.

Then, as on most of the journey to England, I had with me a notebook. I had visited the big library in Johannesburg and copied out a series of Shakespeare speeches, including Henry Vth's response to Westmorland's wish:

'O that we now had here
But one ten thousandth of those men in England
Who do no work today.'
'What's he that wishes so?
My cousin Westmorland? No, my fair cousin:
If we are marked to die, we are enow
To do our country loss. And if to live,
The fewer men, the greater share of honour...'

Over and over again I learned it and a few other famous speeches, which are still part of my mental furniture today.

From Beira I made my way inland, aiming towards Victoria Falls on the Zambezi. Looking at a map now it appears that by air it is 800 miles and by road nearer 1000. Naturally I was still hitch hiking and I remember only one part of the journey to the falls.

A red sports car drew up. The young man driving was in a hurry.

'I'm building a hotel at the Falls,' he said.

The speed limit on the signs at the roadside was 70mph but the driver exceeded it. I watched the speedometer uneasily as it twitched around 90, 95, 100 … I did not expect to survive the journey and it is the only time – so far – that I have ever felt in danger of imminent death. We were together for nearly three hours so I must have been hundreds of miles into that journey before the lift. It is a marvel that he stopped to pick me up at all.

When we arrived, he told me that I could stay there in one of the huts the hotel builders were using. It was just a grass hut but a welcome refuge.

Victoria Falls

Never have I seen a more breath-taking example of nature's terrifying and awesome power, untamed by man. Just look at some pictures somehow. Billions of gallons of water from the Zambezi come thundering over the falls into a great gorge. Misty rainbows fill the air, the sound overwhelms any attempt to speak: you can use only your eyes and ears, striving to take in this stupendous phenomenon.

There is a bridge they have built across the gorge, facing the falls, and I probably walked along it. More intriguing than just staring at the jaw-dropping sight was a path along the riverside, downstream at the base of the gorge. A different kind of glory drew me down there, the mingled dark greens and shades, the depth of the gorge, the tempting path alongside. I walked probably half a mile away from the Falls.

Nairobi

How did I get to Nairobi? Indeed, why did I go there? Certainly, I have a photograph somewhere of a rhinoceros, standing looking towards us about thirty yards from the road. The driver who was taking me had seen it and wanted to show me as well as look himself. The surrounding grass is orange-red, the sun beating down and you can almost feel the heat in the picture.

I think he was taking me to Nairobi. It was there that I had another disconcerting experience displaying my innocence.

I needed a night's lodgings, very cheap. A big woman with a broad grin let me in and I was given a ticket granting me six hours lodgings. Six hours? Puzzled but shrugging, off I went to explore the city. It was the most European of cities, very impressive in its development.

Returning to my lodging, I wanted to go in and leave a bag there. The substantial lady indicated that it was not possible since the room was being used.

Used? I expressed as much outraged anger as I could find but to no avail. Then it dawned on me: it was not a hotel but a brothel.

But I had forgotten another aspect of the journey to Nairobi. While standing by the roadside using my thumb optimistically but with the customary rising despair, a car stopped on the other side of the road, heading back to the Falls. The driver, smiling, told me to hop in.

'I'll take you to Nairobi – not quite all the way but you'll be there quicker than you can imagine.'

Naturally there was nothing to do other than smile, thank and get in. Off we went, first down the main road. Then he turned off onto a track, dusty, sandy and difficult. Even so he seemed to know what he was doing – and I had no choice anyway. It was disconcerting but that was that: I couldn't get out and was, as so often, imprisoned in an unprecedented situation with no rules to guide me.

Half an hour later we stopped beside a small aircraft. To hitch a lift in a passing aircraft going the wrong way was one of the novelties I enjoy remembering, in particular because there was a lesson there: do not assume that everything is as it appears.

We flew to an airfield outside the city and I caught a bus to the centre. I bought an air ticket from Nairobi to Rome the next day. Why Rome and not London? I don't know, but it was my first visit there and remember nothing.

Another chapter: University College library.

When I returned to England I needed somewhere to

live. After an initial landfall, I contacted my old friend Brendan. He and his parents were willing and able to accommodate me for a little while. I stayed there for a few days then found a room to live in near West Croydon Station. Was I working? Maybe…there was a job in the Borough of Wandsworth. I went to see the Librarian in Balham and was taken on as an assistant, essentially shelving books.

Wandsworth and marriage

Wandsworth Libraries provided me with employment for long enough to bring me back to respectability. There was a girl working there whom I was fond of because she was always laughing and rejoiced in life. It was such fun being on the same desk with her and I would have pursued this further if she was not already attached to a boyfriend. What might have been …

A bit later another girl came along. She was an only child and had enterprisingly come to London after taking a librarian's course in Birmingham, her home. She was a nice girl but wanted to break away from her rather imprisoned existence and possibly her domineering father in Sheldon, a Birmingham semi-detached suburb.

Meanwhile Brendan had decided that he was going to become a qualified librarian as well after working in Wallington library and took up a one-year, post-graduate course in Aberystwyth.

It was an unprecedented situation. There we were,

both lonely people in a big city and accordingly thrown together. I was, and remain, a Catholic and after a number of conversations about religion in practice and principle she decided that she would become a Catholic as well. She took instruction from our local Parish Priest and we were married four years later – the same year that I took my degree in Classics.

We embarked on a 'honeymoon' in Shropshire, I think, and I was greatly encouraged that she was happy to hire a bicycle so that we could get around the local villages. We didn't go far but it seemed promising. Cycling and singing in choirs have always been central to my life and here was at least one of them now on the cards. It is true that she was not keen on cycling up hills – an understandable concern – nor indeed down them; even so we were going somewhere, I thought.

University College, London, were advertising for a library assistant. I went to see the Chief Librarian, evidently a Classicist.

'You probably agree that learning the Greek *'-mi'* verbs' (a class of verb endings which were not, unfortunately, irregular but conformed to their own complex patterns and were very common indeed because *histemi, tithemi* and *didomi and* their compounds covered various meanings of 'stand', 'put' and 'give') 'is one of the greatest tasks undertaken by Western man…well, we have a job which will suit your abilities and experience.'

And so it proved. During the war – the second world war – a lot of the older books, dating from 17th century to the 20th, had been transferred to the university book store in Egham for safety, having been bombed during several raids. The evidence was still there, with leaves still scorched and crumbling. Evidence of the second failure – the move to Egham, next to the Thames – was also very clear: the store had been overwhelmed by the river somehow and many of the shelves had been flooded, leaving tide, water and mould marks, green, yellow, brown and dusty.

It was my job to re-catalogue all the damaged books, some 2,000 of them, using the unique cataloguing system devised in the 1930's for the library itself and used nowhere else. This also meant trying to restore them to a readable form by prising the pages apart.

I was under the supervision of a sharp and efficient lady called Magda Czigany, a former Hungarian refugee. She knew exactly what she was doing and had to hold in her occasional impatience when I did not understand the point she was making. However, it all worked. I was there for two and a half years, during which time I completed my Classics degree at Birkbeck. It was the perfect job for me, working with Greek and Latin books – and I was the perfect candidate for the job with my current activities, a marvellous coincidence which might almost have been planned, but of course was simply a lucky accident.

It was indeed lucky because it meant that I could continue with my degree at London University while being employed in one of their libraries. The task took two and a half years – exactly the time I needed to be employed.

Birkbeck College

Brendan, a better scholar than I was, had spent a year undertaking an MA at Birkbeck College. Birkbeck was, and is, an integral college of London university, catering for students who are employed full-time and therefore offering lectures in the evening. You end up taking the same exams as full-time students from Kings, UCL and the rest but approach it in a different way, using your wits and every minute of your spare time.

We were being prepared for the full Classics degree, four language papers translating from Greek and Latin into English – two of them 'easy', two of them very difficult indeed, then two papers translating from English into the other languages, papers on Greek and Roman history, one general paper on classical culture – which I scraped through by one mark – one paper on Greek philosophy…there must have been a couple more since there were twelve in all. Although it was part-time for three years, I was allowed to study full-time for the fourth year on the grounds that I had not taken a full year's grant when I was at Hull and could still claim my grant. This was a luxury, and in truth I did less work, in proportion, in my last year than in the other part-time years.

The lecturers were variable. The head of department was Robert Browning, a gentle, sharp Scotsman with an enigmatic smile, who knew everything. Then there was Brian Caven who taught Roman History, to which I did not respond well. The most colourful character was a man of outstanding self-importance, who would regularly school his students, many of whom were older than he was, into the required responses:

'And what happens to students who are taught by Professor Doctor Doctor' – thus encompassing his full range of degrees – 'Giuseppe Giangrande?'

'They pass!' replied the chorus.

'And what happens if they are not?'

'They fail!' came the dutiful response.

Fortunately, this stuffed pillow of an academic never swum into my personal ken.

The best experience was with Mr A.G. Way, a meticulously careful teacher with a very acute mind and pencils sharp enough to match it. He taught us Greek prose composition with outstanding patience. He would return our efforts with alert, clear, scholarly handwriting neatly and scrupulously scribed, correcting errors with great care and courtesy. I felt ashamed to offer my errors to him.

One of the most important experiences came in my final exams. The last paper was the difficult Greek prose translation, probably Thucydides. I had managed reasonably well the first three passages but was baffled by the last, unable to make anything of it, struggling with some abstruse vocabulary but overall failing to see the point. There were five minutes to go when I just sighed and gave up – and it was this act of relaxation, of shrugging and giving myself over to fate, of letting the mind drift, that did the trick. It came out of the blue but there it was. In tremendous excitement I saw it all and wrote it all out again in great haste but with reasonable accuracy. Again, this was a lesson later on transferred to other pupils: don't get too worried – just relax and let go: it might just happen. It isn't magic and it might not work but it could: if you're going to give up, relax about it. The decision is made, take it easy and see what happens next. Professor Browning, when going through my performance later, said that I had done pretty well in that paper, had just about scraped through the Greek and Roma politics paper – he implied that they had had to add some generous marks to push me over the edge – and managed a 'super-first' in the general Classics paper.

Life and death

During this student period I had to cycle three nights a week from Balham almost to Euston, where Birkbeck College lay. It was the happiest time of my life up to that point because I was overwhelmed by tasks, thinking, the demands of work and study tripping over each other, interspersed with brewing and drinking beer. Was there a time when I thought it all too much? No: it was the deal; the diet and I could see nothing beyond it.

A devastating blow had struck me during the degree. At UCL someone called me to the telephone.

'Is that Anthony?' asked the South African lady, pronouncing my name 'Intony'. 'I'm afraid I have some bad news for you. Your father has passed away.'

It was an impossible moment. I went and sat on the stairs, trying to make sense of it. The best way to explain it is this. Imagine that you have been protected from the cold night air, surrounded by walls which you take for granted will always be there. Suddenly the walls are blown away and you are exposed to the vast, cold, starry night air, the whole universe out there, no protection any more. That is how it felt. Once your father has gone you have to take up his position in the world because there is a vacancy, though you don't necessarily realise it at the time.

It had been five or six years since I had seen him, waving goodbye as I walked away from his flat in Pinetown, Natal. One resolve I had taken then was not to shave my upper lip until I saw him again – and so I have had a moustache for nearly fifty years. He died, it seems, of a 'myocardial infarction', which means a heart attack of some kind, brought about by a life of smoking, drinking a bit too much and sitting rather than walking; he was an inveterate car driver.

Career

It was clear that I had to become something more or less professional and reluctantly decided to enter the teaching profession. I had gone to Professor Browning for a discussion on what might happen after the degree.

'You could teach,' he said.

'Why would I do that?'

'Well, someone has to,' he wryly remarked. At that time the National Curriculum had not been introduced, so that schools had as much freedom as they wished to teach subjects they valued. There were therefore more Classics posts available than there are now, since the subjects involved are taught now only in private, or public, schools. It was only later that the National Curriculum excluded Classics, on the grounds that there were not enough teachers to provide the subject for all the schools in the country, so that it could not be universal. Anyway, who needs Classics when Design Technology is so crucial for everyone?

Plymouth and Devonport

I was given a teaching job in Plymouth, at Devonport High School for Boys, regarded as the best grammar school in the city – they were one of the last authorities to maintain the grammar school system. Two years we were there, just along the road from the school, which was housed in what used to be the naval hospital: the history department occupied the operating theatre.

We used to walk down to The Hoe a lot and all around the city, while I used to go off on trips to anywhere within reach. We went up to Dartmoor once – I think that was just me on my bike – and peered over at the vast grey sprawl that was Dartmoor Prison. There was a lovely lighthouse on the Hoe.

While we were in Plymouth our first son, Thomas, was born. We used to go to Mass in the cathedral every Sunday and it was there that he was baptised.

The house was in a terrace with a tiny garden and a small flat roof. Why cannot I remember its name? Wimpole Street? Winchmore? Wilton Street! From the roof you could just make out the dockyard a mile away and the ships on the stretch of water called the Hamoaze (pronounced 'Hamoize'), the great estuary of the river Plym. I grew red peppers there on the roof: it was warmer than south-east England and a nice place to be, with a low rim of a wall around it. The little garden three floors below had a gate in the wall at the back, leading into an alley between the two roads of houses.

One Sunday morning there was a knock on the front door and there outside stood an American couple. Most apologetically they told us that they were visiting England and that the wife's parents used to live in that very house. Would we very much mind if they came in and had a look at it? We were happy to oblige and they beamed cheerfully to see all the features which the parents had described to them, for the house had changed little in fifty years.

While I did not mind the school or the road, the city itself was not for me, or us, really. The academic standards of the school were very high and it was an excellent start to teaching. However, I could see no prospects of promotion in the school itself – the Head of Department was young and busy – I went to see the Classics advisor to ask him what sort of prospects there were for me in Plymouth.

'Well, we're going to see a Head of Classics job in a few years' time in Okehampton,' he reassured me.

This was enough: I wasn't going to hang around in a town I didn't care for to await the prospects of a job living in an even smaller town forty miles away north of Dartmoor. The Times Education Supplement came into play. I applied nowhere until I was certain, and one day there was an advert for an assistant Classics teacher at St Ignatius College, Enfield. I wrote at some length to Fr Forrester, the Headmaster, telling him at great length, and with utter honesty, that I was very keen indeed to teach in a Catholic school on the grounds that it simply made sense, as an extension of my identity.

Fr Forrester and St Ignatius

One Sunday evening a week later there came a phone call.

'Good evening. Is that Mr Holbourn?' came the alert, scholarly, Glaswegian voice. 'This is Fr

Forrester from St Ignatius College. I wonder if I could ask you a few questions?'

He did. Indeed, he interviewed me for forty minutes, questioning me very closely on everything that was going to matter.

'Very well. Please come for interview on Tuesday morning,' he instructed.

On Tuesday he ran the interview again for another forty minutes. Two more candidates were given twenty minutes each but another had forty minutes as well.

'If we were to offer you the job, would you take it?' I said, yes, I would, instantly thinking that he was also preparing to say 'Well, we're not going to offer it to you.' However, he did, only remarking that another candidate had given me a close run. I never knew what made the difference. My academic career had been pretty feeble, as must be clear from above, with low grades only redeemed by my ultimate success in A-level Greek, for which I had attained a B, having re-taken it, along with Ancient History in my spare time. The level of my degree was just a bit more than adequate, a 2:1.

It was always a pleasure to listen to Fr Forrester, who was clearly going to grill me very incisively. His diction, his grammatical and syntactical command, were exemplary and a joy to hear as he unwrapped his thinking. He knew how he was going to express himself with scrupulous exactitude and he was manifestly a Classical scholar himself.

Balham

While working for Wandsworth Libraries I struck up a friendship with the music librarian at Balham, where I was based most of the time. He was a middle-aged single man who was a most personable and friendly colleague. I used to spend a couple of days a week helping out in the music library. The system was this: in the shelf stacks were the record sleeves, which borrowers would bring to the issue desk. We would find the record from the drawers behind us then slip them into the sleeves. We also examined every returned record for damage. One of the scenarios I longed for, and almost contrived to occur, was a mistaken issue, so that I would deliberately put the wrong records in a sleeve of Russian music. When the borrower returned the Glazunov sleeve containing the Polotsvian Dances I would apologise for my mistake and say, 'It happens occasionally: Borodin error.'

Francis needed a lodger in his house in Byrne Road.

'The only thing I need tell you,' said the librarian-landlord nervously, 'is that you might sometimes hear people come and go in the middle of the night…no need for alarm…it's just my way of life.' He was a homosexual with a wide circle of friends.

One of his friends was a big Jamacian, Victor Hall, with a vast smile and six children. He came into the library one day highly elated, with the news that his wife was pregnant again and they were going to have a boy, he thought.

'What name do you think I should call him?' he asked. I'm running out of names, you see.'

'I suppose you could call him Albert,' I suggested.

'Albert... Albert Hall...hmm...'

'Or even Royal Albert, maybe.'

In all innocence he beamed happily.

'Royal Albert Hall! Dat's a great name!'

I don't know if there is even now such a man.

We therefore took up as our first residence my flat in Byrne Road. She was the breadwinner, working as a qualified librarian in Wandsworth, while I studied to become a teacher, with the teaching practice at Wimbledon College, as I mentioned above. The year's post-graduate 'study' for the PGCE was a horrible time and almost a waste. We attended a series of lectures. It was evident that the teaching staff at St Mary's, Strawberry Hill were as a rule Catholic – that was its purpose – but that they had different levels of thinking and commitment. One of them, who saw himself as a bit of a wag, once talked to us about Our Lady and the church teachings about her.

'Let's now move on to the doctrine so rightly called The Assumption,' he said, smiling archly.

Most of the lectures were dull and we did not really learn anything. We really wanted to know how to teach – I had thought that this was the purpose of the year – but, as one of them told us,

'We're not here to give you a set of tricks to make you able to teach.'

What?! Then what were we there for? Of course! The Philosophy of Education, the Principles, the Psychiatry, the Sociology – anything but the practice. At least, I thought, they might have given us a few straightforward ideas of what not to do, how to deal with groups of obstreperous and reluctant children, boys who would much prefer to be on the playground enjoying themselves, yelling and playing football – something different from just theory. Probably these lecturers were under some kind of directive from the university to ensure that the studies involved some kind of Higher Thinking.

In your application for teaching practice – the most useful part of the post-graduate teaching year – you could tell them the kind of school you would like to teach in. A big Irishman on the same course, John Hussey, told me that the best thing was to be very specific.

'Just put "Single sex Catholic school run by a religious order"', he said, so I did. This meant it would be either St Benedict's, Ealing, or Wimbledon College, run by the Jesuits. They took into account my living in South London and sent me to Wimbledon College. This was my first encounter with the Jesuit order, an association which subsequently continued until I retired from teaching altogether.

The term's teaching practice at Wimbledon College was the most useful, especially learning a few things about the Jesuits and seeing how tricky and interesting it was trying to teach boys who not only knew more than me but were also better educated. They were very patient and courteous and I was ashamed of wasting their time.

Harlow

The first house we bought after Plymouth was in Harlow, where Tom went to primary school. It was a 'town house', a tall, terraced house, in Brockles Mead, the only place we could afford to live after selling the Plymouth house, situated opposite a home for apparently delinquent boys. We hardly ever saw them. Every morning I would take the bus across to the station and the train to Turkey Street. I didn't mind Harlow: there were views over remoter green meadows a few miles away and we were content there. It was also built on the site of several villages, using them as local centres and linking them with the old lanes, now changed into cycle tracks.

Hoddesdon

When it became clear that there was an easier way to go to St Ignatius, on the 310 bus, we decided to move to Hoddesdon, to an end-of-terrace 19th century house in Duke Street. There we put our latest gift, Alex, in a cot in what we called the study, a little room where I had built bookshelves on as many sides as I could find. There were about

1,000 books altogether up there, and more downstairs. All was fine until Alex grew a little and found not only that he could stand up in his cot but also reach the books on the shelves. This provided him with a pastime, reaching out and pulling them onto the floor. An early thirst for literature? The best part of the next house was what we called the study, in which I built more shelves, many of them surrounding the piano.

This was in a newish, 60's house a few minutes' walk away in a vile road called Goodwood Close. I hated it from the moment we moved in, a house in a little circuit of dwellings around a cul de sac. I could not wait to get out every morning and kept away for as long as I could.

We had bought the piano after noticing that Ben was becoming pretty good at playing his little toy piano, so we found a local piano teacher, Miss Octavia Christensen, whom he visited every week for years. Many an evening he would be practising, I with my back to him at a desk on the other side of the little room preparing lessons – not much – marking books and reading.

We never came to know anyone in Goodwood Close in nearly 30 years. I am an affable enough person and spoke to most people but there was no interest. Accordingly whatever friendships I made were at school. We had no car and never would do so I used the garage for my bike, while every other house had two, three or four cars, none of which was kept in the garages. My wife came to know a few people from the school gate at St Augustine's, which provided a good start for the boys.

I embarked on a long and joyous career at St Ignatius. The school was then on two sites, one in Enfield West consisting of the first two years of secondary – years seven and eight now – and the main school in Turkey Street on the A10. I had to commute on two days a week, Tuesday and Friday, from the Lower to the Upper school – a unique position – while two other teachers dealt with Latin and Classical Civilisation on both sites. The Head of Classics, Michael Gunningham, was a distinguished Classicist and the author of assorted books as well as editor of a series of books on Greek and Roman themes. I remember a few moments of interest from being shown round. The lugubrious man who showed me round the Upper School pointed out the label above one of the classrooms:

'Classics Base', it said grandly.

'In what way does the Classics Base differ from the other rooms?' I asked him.

'The name,' he replied. He was correct. Modern Languages, History – they were all there. It was only the Science labs that differed, in having equipment. In fact, we taught in assorted rooms, while sixth form classes were taught on the top floor, where the Head of 6th, Michael Gilbert, had his office. There was also a snooker table there and he would exploit the playing of snooker during study periods by totting up the points on the balls remaining on the table and exacting an equivalent fine, with the funds being given to a local charity – usually St Elizabeth's Home, Much Hadham, close to where he lived. St Elizabeth's is a home for people, most of them young, who suffer from very severe epilepsy.

As we went round the school Michael Gunningham introduced me to another man hurrying by. As he approached Michael said, 'Here comes one of the nicest men you will ever meet.' He was right: it was Kevin Queally, a colleague after that for many years and still a fellow-parishioner here in Hertford. It seems then that I have known him for more than forty years.

They gave me some pastoral experience by putting me first in charge of a 1st year group – year 7 – and then it fell to me to take over as head of the year – or line, as the Jesuits call their year-groups. This role I held for nine years and both Tom and Ben, the first two sons, were in one or other of those groups. One of my main initial concerns was having Tom in the year group. After hours of thinking out how this would work, I first came to the obvious conclusion that I should treat him as just one of the pupils but I knew that this wasn't good enough. A moment later light dawned: of course! What I had to do was to treat every one of the group as if they were my own sons. It was more a matter of attitude than any practical ideas but it seemed to work and felt much better: you were, after all, *in loco parentis*.

The same applied later when I became Head of 6th. Before this I had a 6th form registration group of mixed lads. The groups in the 6th were either A-level students or 'Remove' – boys who had done too poorly in their O-levels to qualify for A-levels and were trying again. They also gave me one of the 'Remove' teaching groups – Classics – about sixteen of them. They were a very mixed bunch indeed, one or two obnoxious, a few quiet and optimistic, all direct and straightforward. Mr Gunningham gave me a syllabus and some books and I got on with the job of teaching them.

I learned more about the Classical world in that year than I had ever known before. The syllabus required that you teach Art and Architecture, about which I knew nothing at all, so I learnt very thoroughly about the Parthenon and its frieze, the Temple of Zeus at Olympia, Ionic and Doric architecture and the history of their development, the layout of the whole Athenian Acropolis and every building on it, and its meaning – everything relevant to the subject. Later on, it became a staple diet in my teaching and I still   have the notes I made, the books I had to buy and the sets of ideas in my head – so thoroughly, indeed, that I can even now deliver a reasonable lecture on it all, supposing anyone were interested. Indeed, I did so last year to our local University of the Third Age. There was also literature but I can't remember what we did – some Greek tragedies, I think, probably Oedipus the King and the Theban plays.

Since it mattered to keep ahead of the boys I had to

be organised; and, for the first time in the history of the school, every one of the group passed at the end of the year. I still don't know why and certainly did not expect it.

Some of them went on to A-level. Few names remain, though I remember Kevin Winkle, a tall, curly headed lad who did reasonably well. D? B? I wonder what happened to him?

At all events the employment at St Ignatius continued, for some three decades, I think. We had contrived three sons – one of them in Plymouth, one in Balham, one in Hoddesdon. Our principles in helping them to grow up were never laid down in books but emerged from who we were. As the woman in charge of them from their babyhood, their mother had the earliest authority over them as she cared for them. I was the bloke who paid the mortgage, came home at night and amiably helped out a bit. I do remember singing 'How Sweet to be a Sloth' to Tom when he was an infant, as a lullaby to send him to sleep, with some success.

There were about four years between their births and you might suppose that it had been planned that way. It had not.

It must have been at about this point that another significant event occurred. Brendan and I were in his flat in Walthamstow, comparing various translation of the Greek New Testament, using a range of translations and versions. It was fairly intense but very interesting. Had I stayed overnight?

Perhaps, because the previous day we had spent hours in the sun varnishing a table.

At all events, there we were reading intensely and thoughtfully. The next thing I knew was coming to, lying on the floor on one side of the room; the table we had been working at was on the other side, with the chair on the floor. Brendan was still seated on his chair, looking utterly bewildered.

We had some tea and talked it over. The best explanation was that the heat and the varnish had somehow got into my head – but it was all guesswork.

A few days later I was crossing a road from the station to the school, presumably in my first year there. The next thing I knew was that I was lying on my back in the road, having blacked out and collapsed, banging my head on the kerb. A car had slowed down to take the corner and therefore did not hit me.

This is a confused reflection since it may be mixed up with a third occasion. That time they took me to a man in a white coat in an office – I think it must have been at Strawberry Hill – who looked me over and said:

'Nothing to worry about. It's the kind of thing that happens to people of your build.' He meant slim.

Only later did I think, 'Who was that man? He was making it up! He hadn't a clue! My *build*? What rubbish!'

My GP sent me to a lady called Dr Monroe, in Wimbledon, I think. She had me undergo a scan, which revealed an odd pattern of gaps in the print-out.

'There you are,' she said, 'Just the pattern we would expect of someone who has epilepsy.' I asked her if I might keep the printout so that I might refer to it in future but it was disconcerting a week later to find that it had become completely blank.

This was entirely unexpected. The asked me if there was any history in the family and I remembered that my father was always talking about taking his pheno-barbitone. They said that this was indeed a drug which might be used to control epilepsy – though we knew nothing of this when we were children.

Various drugs were prescribed, all of which had side-effects of an uncomfortable kind. It was not until years later that a different approach was devised. I have been to many specialists who prescribed various treatments but at last, a very close friend of mine looked into it all and discovered that the best man in the country dealing with epilepsy was Dr Alex Everitt, at St Mary's Hospital in Paddington. We got in touch with him and went to see him. He tried out assorted medications after learning what had failed to work, and at last lit upon the correct and effective balance. I have been taking the same doses for years now – perhaps five years.

There were two other episodes before it was settled. One was on a boat on the Danube, as a result of which the captain had me taken off to hospital. They were going to keep me there but I told the lady doctor that if they did not take the tubes out of my arm straight away, I would tear them out myself and simply walk away: the boat was due to leave again the next day and we would have been left behind. Anyway, I was feeling fine. 'I sink I understand,' said the patient lady doctor, and gave in.

The second was in the foyer of Broxbourne station when I was on the point of catching a train to Nottingham for a national conference, I think for the U3A – I had inadvertently become the chairman of the Hertford group by then.

Evidently this condition can be hereditary and I naturally have wondered whether any of my own sons have undergone anything similar but nothing has emerged yet. It is said that epilepsy usually appears in the late teenage years; but I was 28.

I used to cycle a lot – I still do – and bought a child's seat to attach at the back. Tom was my first passenger and I think he rejoiced in the experience, for recently he has acquired a similar contraption for his own bike to take Nadia around. Cycling has always been part of life and, as I say, I had expected that my wife would carry on cycling. It was not to be.

'I'll get you a bike.'

'No, don't.'

'Why?'

'I'm frightened of the traffic.'

Well, we could walk up to the river bank and then cycle along the river bank – it's a good, wide track.'

'I might fall off and fall in.'

This conversation went on in the same way and was fruitless. I therefore used to go off cycling by myself.

The other major factor in life was singing, mostly in choirs. I had already joined the church choir as well as another one, run by the man who had been Alex' piano teacher. Then a momentous event took place. In Hertford one day I ran into Gill Gifkins, the lady who had taught my son violin for a few years.

'Oh, you must come and join our singing group!' she said in her customarily enthusiastic way.

'Must I?'

'Yes! Here are the details…'

I did.

The lady who ran the choir in Hertford Heath was a very clear-headed and capable musician but also very interested in words. She once sent me an e-mail in reply to a message I had sent asking about the music. There had been some dispute with another member of the choir about the pronunciation of a particular Latin phrase.

This led to a sequence of messages dealing with words, spelling, meaning, thoughts, ideas – all sorts of things. It was becoming clear that we were communicating along the same lines. A major factor was the spelling of 'sigmoidoscopy'.

In addition, I bought a high-quality keyboard for use at the Hall in Hertford Heath, to use instead of the awful piano there. However, it was very heavy and I undertook to come over and put it in the car on Wednesday mornings. Subsequently it seemed sensible to come over on Tuesday evenings and nights.

'Come and join the choir in Broxbourne, I had previously suggested to my wife.

'I can't sing.'

'Yes, you can, I've heard you.'

'But I can't read music.'

'You don't have to…'

… and so on and on.

Again, I had to go on my own. If she had been prepared to come along to these activities, the choir or cycling, or even one of them, life might have emerged in a different way since we would have been doing something together.

School

The journey to Enfield was always undertaken on the 310 bus. The first bus left Hoddesdon bus stop at about 6.30 so that I was able to arrive at Turkey Street at the same time as the caretaker and the cleaners. Indeed, I usually opened the building for Penny, the cleaner, and we enjoyed coffee together. This was when I had taken over as Head of 6th Form in a building called Roselands, formerly the house occupied by the Jesuit priests who were a major part of the school. Indeed, some still lived in the house next door.

I had an office on the ground floor but there was a fine balcony overlooking the garden. The roses in the garden were lovely and I used to trim them both before and after school, so that the process was similar to carving a living sculpture: whatever you did to a rose affected the way it grew. This was a new idea to me and most instructive.

How much can I say about Roselands and the fun we had there! We were lucky enough to have a Sixth Form Secretary, Cathy Bates, who had an office next door to mine. She was a lovely person who developed a cheerful, intelligent and sensitive relationship with the boys, far more than a secretary. She was also efficient and kind to me, gently pointing out things that needed doing or might be done better. This was the second half of a long pastoral career, since nine years before that, the Headmaster, Michael Blundell, had called me.

I had formerly been a tutor in the First Year, later known as Year seven. The Headmaster, Michael Blundell, once called me in to his office one Friday afternoon and sat me down.

'In your wildest dreams,' he said, 'Had you ever considered being the First Year Line Master?'

I was astonished. 'No,' I replied.

'Well?'

'Er … I could do with a bit of time to think about it.'

'Let me know on Monday.'

If I accepted it would mean – though I did not think about it at the time – that Ben, having been in the First year under my pastoral tutelage, would fall beneath my shadow for a further two years in the sixth form. That is what happened and it worked, even when he became my A-level Latin class.

It is important to observe how crucial Michael was in my own development in the college. We had some things in common, the most obvious of which was a fairly conservative view about orthodox Catholicism. He was, and remains, a highly intelligent man, a Geography teacher with a genuine regard for Classics at all levels. He had an astonishingly detailed mind: he knew all the boys and their names, their addresses, their primary schools – I sometimes thought that he knew the names of their cats as well. He had all this to hand largely because he spent a lot of time in the playground just talking to the boys and listening to them; having listened to them and, in his deceptively Olympian manner, familiarised himself with as many of them as possible, he retained it all. I suppose that he saw it as a major part of his business as Headmaster simply to be in command of as much information as possible and it certainly increased his authority for every boy in the school saw him as speaking to them individually when addressing the College as a community.

Over the weekend there was some discussion about the possible appointment and we agreed that I might as well have a go, so I said yes. It was clear that a change in approach was needed from the previous post-holder, a strong and perhaps aggressive man who might have appeared insensitive. I was given Gerry Davies as a deputy and we worked well as a team in our different styles. Gerry was a hard man, a PE teacher, a large Rugby player, respected and liked but not to be messed with. He was far more intelligent than most people thought and we got on very well for those nine years together. It was a most satisfying business, summed up by our interviews with the parents of naughty boys. Gerry would take the strong line, direct and forceful; my approach was a touch more subtle; parents were sometimes baffled at first but our aim was to let them leave after half an hour or so with a smile on their face and a sense of having been dealt with fairly, all of us having come to a better understanding of what was needed. Occasionally we would come across parents who refused to compromise. I can remember one couple in particular who insisted that the detention awarded to their son was unjust and unfair, and that he was not going to serve it. We differed, of course, and made it very clear to them that our authority was the same as theirs, on the school premises.

'Clearly,' I told them, 'You do not trust the school or the authorities within it. It is obvious that you have one crucial duty to ensure that your son is not unhappy.'

'So, what's that?'

'You must take him away and find another school which will treat him fairly.'

They backed down. There were always a few like that but we did not mind much: it was all part of the job and fair enough, given that we were dealing for the most part with extremely thoughtful and trusting parents.

My favourite time of the week was the so-called Line Assembly. On this occasion it was the Line Master's job to dictate, reprimand, cajole, praise and advise his 180 boys, who were very good at pretending to listen. Gerry and I would share the duties though I was probably too full of words. The boys were patient: they had no choice. What did I talk about? Hard to recall; I wonder if the boys remember now?

The academic arrangements at that time were as follows: when the boys came into the school, they were arranged in assorted bundles applying no criteria of ability or achievement. A reasonable balance was struck over the various classes, assembling them as sensitively as possible on the basis of information provided by those who knew them best and keeping groups from the same primary school together, unless we had learnt that they should not be. I had come to know as many as I could before they arrived by going to visit the primary schools who sent us the greatest numbers – St George's, Enfield, St Edmunds, Edmonton, a good many from Tottenham and a few from here and there. Usually about 20 schools were involved and I tried to go to as many as possible, to meet the top juniors' teachers and learn about the new arrivals.

When parents applied for their sons to attend the school, they were obliged to complete a form indicating that they were practising Catholics, a claim which would be supported by their Parish Priest. Academic excellence was not part of the demand: people who wanted only academic attainment applied to the grammar school, Latymer, in Enfield. Even so we had some very able boys, as well as the extremely weak ones. This was a marvellous mixture and we were a genuinely comprehensive school catering for children of all abilities.

There were 180 places available every year. There came the time when the Governors met to decide how to separate those who could come from those who could not and it was never an exact science but a matter of experience and judgement. I used to attend these meetings as well, even before I was a governor myself. Only the Admissions Committee, half a dozen of them, were present. Hours were spent on the process, trying to get it right, trying to read between the lines and remind ourselves that it was the lines, not what lay between, that gave the information.

The priests' references were sometimes conclusive:

'Thoroughly committed attenders at Mass and wholly involved in parish activities' would give the nod; 'Never seen them, except at Easter and Christmas' sent the application onto another pile.

The team of form tutors met weekly to ensure that we were all following the same standards, according to personality and particular skills, and at first, I was also one of them. It soon became clear that this was a bad arrangement and we agreed that the Line Master should not have a form. It was a joy to hear the views and perceptions of the various tutors and the exchanges of ideas and banter.

Meanwhile I had taken over as Head of Classics as well. It seemed to go pretty well holding both posts but when another tutor, Claire Fearon, joined the school as a Classics teacher a division of roles began to emerge. She had proved herself a gifted and very clear communicator as well as a strong character. I remember once seeing her rebuking a lad who was a foot taller than she was, a bit of a thug. He was backed up against a wall, unable to withstand the onslaught of crisp, irresistible, logical and sequential sentences with which she was peppering him. She was a winner in a most charming way; you did not argue with Claire because she was right.

Following my years as Head of First Year I became Michael Gilbert's deputy in the Sixth Form. I slightly resented this at first since no-one had asked me about it: in the Ignatian tradition it was just done and you complied. It never dawned on me that this was a preparation for the next year: Michael had had enough and retired. I applied for his job and was appointed.

When I took over as Head of Sixth, the whole Sixth Form moved across into Roselands, a large house with its own garden and a balcony overlooking the roses. Roselands had formerly been the home of the Jesuit community but their numbers had dwindled: they did not need a building as large as Roselands, whereas it was ideal as a home for the two hundred sixth formers and staff. The nine years I spent there were joyous.

I used to play games with the boys constantly. We would play The Animal Game: I would go and join a group of friends, and one of us would straight away say 'Aardvark' or 'Antelope'. The one to his left just had to say 'Bear', the next 'Cat', and so on, until we got round to the A again and we had to find another animal not yet mentioned. It never lasted more than five minutes, then I would go away. Still, we laughed a lot. I learned a lot about teaching and relationships, constantly. It would be overstating it to claim that many of the boys were in effect friends but it was fairly close to that.

There were various clubs founded. The SVP was not, as some thought, the St Vincent de Paul Society but the Society for the Verification of Proverbs, an idea I remembered from listening to Frank Muir years before. We would meet more or less weekly and propose a saying. For example, did too many cooks spoil the broth? Was there any point in crying over spilt milk? What actually happened when you put a bull in a China shop? At weekly Sixth Form assemblies the leader of the group would report on our investigations to the bemused sixth form. I remember that we concluded that there was indeed a point in crying over spilt milk but the amount of milk was crucial. You had to have many, many tears to make the wiping up effective so you had to ensure that there was a lot of crying done. To bring this about you needed to have at least fifty people weeping into little bowls; there had to be a bowl-collector. But how could you ensure that they were all shedding tears? Clearly, they had to be genuinely moved, either to sadness or laughter. Making people unhappy was ethically wrong so it had to be laughter, leading to the conclusion that you would need to interview a series of comedians. The reader will see that there was no end to the thinking we did, essentially to entertain but also to enrich the way that the boys looked at the world, their perspective on life. Certainly, this worked while we were together but there is no evidence that it lasted into their adult lives.

Then there was the Sesquipedalian Society, a group who were determined to use words as long as possible.

I will spare the reader any more anecdotes. Ah yes! The HIT Squad! Boys who had been particularly tricky were appointed to the HIT Squad and a notice was put on the board in large letters informing every one of the honour. The Horticultural Improvement Team were needed to weed the gardens, dust the tables and chairs, sweep the terrace and so on, all after school when everyone else was on their way home.

At the time there was in the news the plan to issue ASBOs – Anti-Social Behaviour Orders. This, too, gave us food for thought and we devised RASBOs. Every week the fortunate winners of RASBOs had their names listed on the notice board, with the reasons for their good fortune – running along corridors, damaging paintwork, throwing books across the room – I can't remember now any of the specifics. However, these Roselands Anti-Social Behaviour Orders caused much glee as well, though there was no competition for their acquisition; however, it was different from the punishments in the main school – as were most things.

It was important to have a capable and sympathetic Deputy. There was no advertisement: I just appointed someone, probably because Michael expected it. It was a young man called James Jeffery, a teacher of Business Studies, intelligent, very able, very clear in any exposition, entirely understanding of my own agenda and above all relaxed, good-humoured and trusted by the boys. We sat in the Roselands garden one day under a tree one day after the agreement had been made. I was disconcerted when he asked me, 'What would you like me to do?'

'Well, whatever you would like to do. We'll work it out,' I replied, reflecting that I should have thought about it but also thinking that I needed him there because of his personality and qualities, not because I wanted anything particular done. At all events, he was happy to go along with it and chip in appropriately at assemblies.

Then there was David Maxim, another Business Studies teacher about whom many rumours were circulated. It was widely believed that he was a millionaire, a man who had made his money in oil and was now giving back to society by teaching the practicalities of business. We were happy to encourage the rumour, largely by strenuously denying it:

'What? Do you really suppose that that Mr Maxim leaves his mansion in Essex every day, jumps into his other car and leaves the Bentley at home, just to come in and waste his time trying to get you lot through your exams? You overestimate your value, young man…'

Strictly speaking I was supposed to offer some sort of careers advice to these young men who were with a year or so of leaving school. There was a proper careers department, very capable and experienced, but because I had to write all the UCAS references – the references for people applying to university – it was important to be involved in their futures in as many ways as possible. You could not simply write them off and wave them goodbye. In fact, the only advice I was able to give them went something like this:

'You must appreciate that I have failed many times over in my life, and you are allowed to do so and yet survive. Indeed, failure is one of the best routes to success. We all know people who passed all their exams with A's; we also know others who struggled to reach this level at all yet succeeded after a few tries. Don't worry about failing – just don't *try* to fail. It only works if you fail against the odds.'

Here is the advice.

- 'First, if you get a job, keep it. Turn up at the right time, stay there until it's time to go or longer and do what you're meant to do.
- 'Second, be a nice bloke. Get on with the people you work with. Most of you are good at that anyway, if nothing else.
- 'Third – and this is probably more important, just, than the others. If you wake up in the morning knowing that you are going to spend your day doing things which are a natural extension of who you are, you will be a happy man. If you know that it is going to be a struggle keeping your mind on a job you don't really care about, you will be unhappy.'

Throughout the time when Michael Blundell was Head, his deputy was Paul Adams, a thoroughly decent, quick, sympathetic and intelligent former Head of Sixth in another school, a man whose integrity was beyond question. We got on very well, having a similar perception of humanity and the world. He used to spend his summers umpiring round the country in Minor Counties cricket matches and he knew exactly how things worked. He was Michael's natural successor as head.

One of Paul's many distinctions was to have taught Russian for years at Campion School – his degree was in French and Russian. The idea of introducing Russian to St Ignatius was attractive but impractical. However, when one of the History teachers wanted to organise a sixth form trip to Russia partly in support of the syllabus she was teaching, he was very supportive. He was unable to come but I was asked to go along, since I was a member of the SMUT / SLUT – Senior Management Team/Senior Leadership Team. Helen Skilton said that she wanted to take a 'heavy' along to wield a bit of authority where necessary. My 10 stone 7 was evidently sufficient to justify this description.

I would love to say much more about the trip to Moscow and St Petersburg. The night, for example, when our group returned to the hotel in breathless panic, having been chased across Red Square by a group of Russian thugs; the morning when I walked out on the ice covering the Baltic Sea, fifty yards from the beach, the ice thick enough to support the weight of a car fifty yards further out. It had been good learning a bit of Russian in advance: my thought was that it would be better to learn something, even a few phrases and the alphabet, just to appear ahead of the boys. The absolutely breath-taking glory of most of the churches was one thing that struck us: when we went into one, we gazed at the altar and our eyes went up, and up, and up to the dazzling gold of the vast altarpiece. As Helen observed, it was quite literally jaw-droppingly beautiful: our eyes lifted and our lower jaws stayed in place so that we were open-mouthed in astonishment. One of the revelations about the country came when we visited some of the palaces, indescribably ornate, unbelievably opulent. One of us spoke what all of us felt: it was no surprise that there had been a revolution, so vast was the chasm between the wealthy and the peasants.

Some pages ago I talked about the beginnings of epilepsy. This has been a persistent companion for more than forty years now but such is the expertise of the medical experts involved that it has caused problems only occasionally. For years I continued to take the same medication which seemed to do the trick. What mattered, it seemed, was concentration: I never had an 'episode' when I was in the classroom, a situation which demanded full attention and close focus in case. The boys were always on the edge of getting the better of you; you could not relax, though it was helpful to appear so, and the whole performance demanded sharp focus to keep thinking, to maintain the tricks of presentation, so the illness never had a chance to get in. In a similar way I have never had an attack when cycling, though often speculated on what would happen if I did. Occasionally there were 'auras', a vague sensation that Something was lurking just out of sight and beyond reach, as though some venomous beast were growling in the background. These 'auras' often occurred at weekends or in the holidays – indeed, exclusively – and usually on Saturday mornings, or when tensions built up. These occasions did become more frequent later, but we will deal with them as they occurred. The medication was by and large successful but did not really settle down until fairly recently, the last seven or eight years. In some ways I miss the occasional episodes, for the illness seemed to me rather like a little pet, a small dog which was usually under control but occasionally became snappy and bit my heels.

Cricket

A substantial part of my life has been involved in cricket at a pretty low level. Patrick and I became obsessed by the game in 1963, the year when the West Indians came to play. We loved them all – Basil Butcher, Seymour Nurse, Rohan Kanhai, Gary Sobers – we hated it when his name was spelt with two R's, since his name was Garfield and Gary – the off spinner whose name I have forgotten, the wicket keeper Deryck Murray and the two huge fast bowlers Wes Hall and Charlie Griffith. Hall was tall and elegant but ferocious, a man who relied on a natural skill. Griffith was a different kind, grim, gruesome, hostile.

We also remembered – though from legend – the 1950(I think) West Indies team led by Trevor Goddard, the team which defeated us memorably, largely through the amazing skills of their two spin bowlers, Sonny Ramadhin and Alf Valentine. Ramadhin was still playing years later for Lancashire but I don't know what happened to Valentine.

'Yardley tried his best,
But Goddard won the test,
They gave the crowd plenty fun,
Second Test and West Indies won,
With those little pals of mine,
Ramadhin and Valentine.'

The calypso by Lord Beginner, with his chorus joining in on the last two lines, was magic and unforgettable.

When I was still at school as a child, we had Games on Wednesday afternoon. In the summer term it was cricket. One Wednesday we were playing – I was about fourteen – and the teacher, knowing that I was too weak, my arm too feeble, to return the ball more than a few yards, put me at second slip for protection from humiliation. A boy called Wainwright was bowling, faster than anyone else in our year, and I was crouched there, knees bent, trying to look right and hoping that I would have to do nothing. He bowled; the batsman edged it. That is all I remember until finding myself lying on the ground with the ball in my right hand – and I am left-handed. The unprecedented cheers, applause and admiration made me glow, more with embarrassment than pride, for I had done nothing: it just happened.

Thenceforth I was seen as a potential cricketer and have remained just that for the last 60 years. I love the game for countless reasons. I love dressing up and looking the part without having to expose my thin legs and scrawny arms. I love the incredible truth that there is a place for anyone, however incompetent, on a cricket field, even if it is backstop in case the wicket keeper misses it. It was always shameful but inevitable to hear the captain shout 'Back him up!' when, having run towards the boundary and flung the ball with every ounce of effort I had towards – roughly – the wicket-keeper, its gentle parabola was clearly taking it no more than a pitch length: it needed someone half-way to collect the ball and complete the process.

The truth is that I have never seen anyone on a cricket field as incompetent as I was, except perhaps my brother Patrick. What we brought to the game was twice as much gusto and enthusiasm as the rest of the team put together. I can remember at school that there were plenty of members of the 1st XI who were in all the school teams; it was taken for granted that they would do so because they were athletic and ball-sensitive – but they did not love the game, just played it. Mick Ogilvie, for example, was tall, dark, well-built and given to twitching the corner of his mouth in a way which, doubtless, made girls weak at the knees in admiration for his physique. He could do anything but, unlike us, it did not matter to him at all.

Patrick and I saw ourselves as bowlers. At any rate when a new captain asked us what I did, my answer was 'Well, I don't bat.' I can't remember whether Patrick was a better bat than I was but it would not be difficult. He tried to bowl leg-spin and genuinely studied the art, the grip, the theory, genuinely admired the real ones. He could make the ball spin all right, but not on a length: neither of us had the control to pitch it correctly unless by accident.

'What do you bowl?' the captain would ask.

'Slow left arm,' I replied confidently, knowing that none of these words were untruthful. I could make the ball spin and whirr in my upturned hand, using the index finger to impart a ferocious buzzing. I could let it fall to the grass and – ping! – off it would bound to the left, just as it ought. Alas, when the arm came over, I had no way of sensing or determining how to make it land at the right place rather than a few yards in front of me, a yard outside the stumps or even sailing over the wicket-keeper's head far beyond his reach.

I did sometimes bowl out of the back of the hand, the delivery known as a Chinaman, partly to bamboozle the batsman and partly to provide an excuse for inaccuracy, but it was disastrous.

On reflection I know that my best bowling figures in a real match, with real players were something like 3-20, though I know not how it happened. I do remember once beating the bat with one that turned, an occasion which again made me think that I could actually do it, like the catch. As Ken Barrington once said, 'If we could do every time what we can do occasionally, we would all be brilliant.'

As a batsman they cautiously put me in at no.7 – a nowhere position where someone might or might not make a small impact. Later I offered to open the batting facing the opening fast bowlers, and, given the chance, have always offered to do so since. This is nothing to do with aptitude or skill but a facet of my character. I am impulsive and foolhardy and I enjoy having a go at doing things which others might hesitate over. Probably it is because, essentially, I have nothing to lose – my average won't get any worse – and possibly something to gain, either in reputation or possibly a couple of nicks off the edge for four. You had to wear all the appropriate protective gear so there was not much chance of being hurt.

On the rugby field – I will not say as a rugby player – I was of limited use for a couple of games, just a keen and determined winger. One vivid memory is indelible.

The opposing winger, fast, big, strong, muscular, was thundering towards our line with the ball. 'Tackle him!' yelled the captain, so I did, not wishing to appear reluctant. I had seen others do it so I flung both arms round the top of his vast legs – I knew the rules – and down he went. It was a moment of triumph, never repeated.

The highest score I ever made was 13. I could not

hit the ball off the square and simply put the bat roughly there and hoped it would rebound somewhere. Yet one day, while playing for Dulwich Drifters, an itinerant side with no ground and no money, captained by one Malcolm Parfitt, I hit a six; well, I scored six from one ball, anyway. My brother saw it on the scorecard the following week and could not believe it. We used to play on alternate Saturdays since they could not afford to have us both in the same team. I explained to him how it had happened. A quickish bowler bowled, the ball bounced just outside the leg stump, I swivelled to watch it, the ball hit the top of the bat as I turned and rebounded in the air to land over the short boundary a few yards away. There it was in the scorebook.

Later, when I became a teacher, I was allowed to 'manage' the U12 XI. There are few memories of those days and perhaps few games down there in Plymouth at Devonport High School, where I was taken on to teach Classics, though I can remember the names of our opening bowlers, Clive Swiggs and Keith Apps. I was allowed to play a game for the Staff XI, captained by my Head of Department Alan Wroath, a superb cricketer as well, a man who could do anything. The best outcome was that I had to umpire a lot and thoroughly enjoyed it, especially because if you made a mistake, you were never wrong. Indeed, I have enjoyed umpiring here and there for years when needed.

'Managing' a cricket team was not a popular role because it meant devoting virtually your whole

Saturday to the game. My keenness took precedence over my waywardness and inexperience. We were a grammar school but apparently had a tradition of playing all the expensive public schools in the area, schools with superb facilities and often professional coaches.

Later at St Ignatius I played regularly for the staff team. Regularly meant once a year, against the 1st XI. My youngest Alex son emerged as a pretty good cricketer, not as good as the best in the team but essentially a decent bloke whom they all liked and wanted as their captain, probably his best asset, like Mike Brearley. Accordingly, that great moment came when he and I were on opposing sides in the annual Staff v. 1st XI game.

A. Holbourn's XI v. A. Holbourn's XI.

And that, too, was a year with memorable moments. One Saturday we were playing one of the local public schools, a team which came every year to us simply to record yet another victory All they needed to do was turn up, bowl us out for forty or fifty, knock off the runs and have an early afternoon.

I was umpiring when their captain was bowling. He appealed constantly and essentially devalued the process since in his view a hit on the pads was LBW, regardless of the line. I was umpiring at his end and had had enough. Accordingly, when our captain Alex was struck on the back pad, right on middle-and-leg, and their captain wheeled round triumphantly with his customary yell of triumph, I disdained to respond in any way, not even shaking my head. He couldn't believe it.

'Oh, come on, umpire, that was out!'

'Just look in the score book,' I told him.

He could do nothing but fume.

Later, when they were batting, there he was in his lordly fashion, scoring freely. Alex was bowling. The ball hit the batsman on the pad outside the leg stump.

Alex appealed with diffident optimism: up went the finger. The batsman looked at me incredulously but I kept the finger raised: there is no argument with an umpire's decision and off he had to go.

Essentially it was punishment for arrogance and I had no regrets. At the end of the game, I offered my resignation to Bernie Cove, in charge of Games.

'I cheated today,' I told him, 'And I have to resign.'

'Oh, we all do it,' he said. 'Just forget it.'

For years since then, I have been searching in vain for a local team weak enough to let me play. The nearest team play in the field just over the garden fence and one sunny afternoon a couple of years ago I went there during a game.

'Do you play?' asked one of them sitting in the shade of the pavilion steps.

'I have done, but the question is, do you have a team for the elderly and incompetent but eager?'

'We do have a colts' (he did say colts, not clots) 'team, who play on a Sunday.'

Clearly this was no use, so the best I can do is listen to the cries of approbation, despair, dismay and triumph over the hedge during the matches.

All this has returned to my mind because I have been sketching my cricket hat, the same one I wore 55 years ago, probably my oldest possession other than AA's Mah Jongg cards.

These cricket visions and memories enriched my life; the experiences made me face reality and shatter illusions. Yet nothing will ever drive away the pictures with which the inside of my head is papered; a series of colourful, emotional, delightful and moving – in both senses – pictures.

Thus, it is that the scent of new-mown grass, a pavilion, a roped-off square or a field of green peopled by white-clad figures, hold me spellbound. It is magic.

I have said little about religious matters. The truth is that I was baptised as a Catholic, have always been one and will never cease until I die. This was clear from the age of seven, when I made my first Confession and Communion. The concepts of Heaven, Hell and Purgatory have been part of my thinking ever since then, usually making a difference but not always. I am in no doubt that all three of those 'places' exist and that the vast proportion of the human race will have to spend a good deal of 'time' being prepared to enter Heaven. In Elgar's 'Dream of Gerontius', an oratorio ironically written to a text from my old acquaintance Cardinal Newman, the soul of the dying man is accompanied into eternity by his Guardian Angel, who explains what is going on. After the terrifying turmoil of death itself, the music becomes serene, almost sweet and remote. Gerontius says:

'I went to sleep but now I am refreshed...'

The Angel brings him gradually to the throne of God but on the way, he hears the Choir of the Angelicals, the angels who attend Him. It is utterly beautiful music and I dare not say more lest the words used do no justice to it. Only once have I been involved in singing it, with Ware Choral Society. I joined them specifically because I found out that they were singing it.

It is not easy being a Catholic. As Dad once said to me, 'The problem is that you go to Confession and are forgiven by God through the priest but you know it's all going to go wrong.' He eventually stopped going to Mass though always believed it to be the only thing that mattered.

I have been through similar experiences, though in my case I still attend Mass. I cannot take Communion because I cannot go to Confession, entirely because there are three conditions for the forgiveness of sins: contrition (feeling that you're sorry), confession (admitting that you have done wrong) and satisfaction (undertaking the penance imposed by the priest). I can admit my errors and sins and can undertake whatever penance is imposed, but contrition can be only partial.

Yes, I am sorry for any hurt I have caused, but I am in no way sorry for one particular step which I know the Church condemns. On the contrary, it is a cause of joy and I cannot pretend otherwise. As for having a Firm Purpose of Amendment, that is out of the question. How will things work on the Day of Judgement? This is out of my hands now. What is certain is that, even if I were to be abandoned here on earth and left on my own for any reason, I would still have the same view. I could never say 'Oh, I can see now that it was all a big mistake. Sorry!' That would indeed be true hypocrisy (if that is not an oxymoron).

Weekly Mass is still part of my life. People might say that this is hypocrisy as well, but it is not. I am not pretending that I am being good by attending Mass. The Church is full of sinners working towards goodness, well aware of their own inadequacies but needing the pull towards perfection that the Church gently asks. Indeed, my thoughts all the time deal with the powerful tension that exists between doing the right thing and doing what I want and love. This brings me back to Aeneas again with his impossible choice: found Rome or stay with Dido? It is especially true when I hear the homilies and sermons spoken by the priest, sympathetically but clearly reminding me of the impossible problem.

One of the Parish Priests I had, in Hoddesdon, knew me as a pillar of the parish and the schools within it. After all, I had become Chair of Governors in one and Vice-Chair in the other. Because of the ineluctable developments in my life, it became obvious that I could no longer maintain those roles, so I went to him and told him. I could still have maintained the jobs to be done, the genuine and total support of the schools and all that they stood for. Nor was it a matter of scandal: I don't think that I was concerned lest anyone in the parish discover that I was leading a double life: I don't much mind what people think. It was more that if it became a matter of common knowledge then parishioners and parents might well feel let down, and it would not be fair.

I do not know which of us was more embarrassed on that occasion. Fr Philip could not take it or understand it, was lost for words and could not cope. I could not withhold the truth from him, a truth he would never have imagined, and, since he was supposed to be pastorally capable, it seemed that he might have come across the situation before in his fifteen years or so as a priest. Yet, it was too hard for him.

Since then, I have met him here in Hertford at a Deanery Mass and reminded him of that very difficult interview.

'Oh, well, that was a long time ago,' he said. He clearly felt that he had come a good way since then, a surprising reaction.

When I went to our Parish Priest in Hertford and told him, he had a different approach. He looked at me thoughtfully. 'Well, it happens,' he said. We continue to have a good and understanding relationship, though I remain uneasy; not that I wish to be or feel comfortable since relaxing in a cosy chair of complacency will never work.

Cycling

This deserves a separate section all to itself. Bicycles have always been there and have helped to shape life year after year.

My first bicycle was a small green device but I cannot recall when or where I had it – probably in Kenley. Maybe I cycled to school on it.

Then I was lent, on a long-term basis, Brendan's bike, which his father had used to cycle round London on decades before. It was brown, strong and big and I used it confidently for a few years. There must have come a time when I moved on, shamefacedly, to my own second-hand machine. Certainly, in Harlow, I cycled to the station and all around on it, then bought another.

I cannot remember all the machines I have had; there are pictures of assorted bikes I have had, particularly a white hybrid bike I bought about ten years ago and still ride here and there. I even bought one of those small-wheeled contraptions, on Tom's recommendation, but I made the mistake of paying too little: there were only three or four gears on it and I needed seven. I have since passed it on to a friend who takes it on the train to Cambridge and back. The white 'Charge Tap' has eight hub gears, the highest and lowest at each end more extreme than the derailleur on the road bike. It was this one that I used to cycle from Lille to Paris in the company of James Jeffery. We started a sixth form cycling club and led groups here and there, through Epping Forest and the local environs.

The most dramatic occasion happened when a lad called Conor Gaffey, a very bright but ethereal boy, came along with a few others and we were on our way over the Chilterns. As we went over the top, he said to me quietly 'I think my brakes have gone'. They had. He had no option but to whistle ahead of us all into the centre of a town there, overtaking us all.

It was a Saturday lunchtime and we were all seriously alarmed about the outcome but when we reached the high street there was Conor, sitting quietly on his bike. He had hurtled down the hill and arrived in the town, turning left sharply into the traffic and gradually coming to a halt. He was very calm, as ever.

We had always thought that Conor had the angels on his side, for many reasons, and this confirmed our impressions. I don't know what happened to him other than knowing that he was involved in an

English degree somewhere. We had to write a very careful reference for him, taking into account all his strengths and weaknesses.

This sequence of bikes ended up in lots of pretty good machines, ending up – for the time being – in a blue road bike. This evidently means one with tyres which are designed for road rather than rough ground, though I still have the white hybrid used in Belgium and France. The latter was a delight. James and I spent five days cycling to Paris, in, I think, 2012, an account of which has already been composed; perhaps I should include some of it in this tale as well.

The most significant moment on that trip was when we stopped for some reason, then moved on. A few miles further on James said in surprise that he had dropped or lost some device with which he was recording our progress. I suggested that we go back.

'No,' he said, 'It's only a thing.'

This remark has lived in my consciousness ever since.

There was another occasion, when according to the map the canal we were on disappeared beneath a hill.

When we reached the hill, we had two options: either to climb a good way over it or continue along the waterway under the hill. We decided on the latter.

It was a long tunnel, probably nearly a mile, and we could just see a tiny white dot far ahead. If there were lights at all they were not working and the path was no more than two feet wide all the way. I went ahead, very nervous lest the slightest slip on some hidden pebble might send me splashing helplessly into the Stygian waters, never to be seen again. Other creatures scuttled about in the dark and from the ceiling ten feet above hung curtains of webs. What size of spiders could have been responsible for such things? The webs draped themselves over us as we cycled gingerly through the blackness and we imagined the padding of rapid little feet along the walls beside us. When we looked back, there was the tiny light of the tunnel's beginning, it seemed a night-time away.

We reached Paris eventually and cycled round it, crossing bridges and junctions with some trepidation wrapped in foolhardy confidence, sometimes on the correct side of the road. We stayed there for a few days, biking round the city and along the Champs Elysees, the dazzling spine of the city. From the Arc de Triomphe you could see three miles away The Louvre and the unique sight of La Defense and La Pouce. We cycled to La Defense and stood in wonderment. The whole site, set in the business quarter, seems to be a monument to civilisation, with a great hollow steel cube 300 feet high, and The Thumb standing there in the middle of it, about forty feet high. There is no explanation but since it is, apparently, a cast-iron statue of the sculptor's own thumb we may think that it is a representation of the importance of this digit, opposed to the first finger, in the ability of humans to devise tools and make things.

We returned on the Eurostar afterwards but have not, alas, biked together since, despite my attempts to contact James; or perhaps we have and I have got things in the wrong order.

France was a pleasure to bike in. We bowled along great, broad highways, obviously designed to accommodate cyclists, with great poplar trees on each side, up long hills and with the vast countryside stretching away. Cyclists were always treated with respect there. It always felt that France was a huge country by contrast with Britain, though it might not be when you measure it. The *gites* we stayed in were kind and obviously expected people like us.

Another cycling trip I undertook with the Head of Science at Ignatius, Bob Thornton. He was going to visit his daughter in Manchester and had worked out a route there, cycling along the canals and rivers. He wanted, I think, some company and knew that I was a good bet, ready for any interesting enterprise. We met at his home in Watton-at-Stone and discussed it. There was an account I wrote about it but I can't find it: it was called 'Canals and bikes.' But I will have to get some highlights from my memory.

The richest memory I have is from a path near Leicester. So many of the canal-side paths were horribly bumpy, with dried mud making it hard to go at any great speed. Bob was on this occasion in front.

The path was broad usually but occasionally wobbled a bit and dipped towards the river itself. There ahead was such a dip and Bob's front wheel went in, followed by his rear wheel; I followed: in and out went my front wheel…but my rear wheel had other ideas. Down it went and seemed to have a mind of its own, thinking 'Ooooh, this is good – I'll carry on sliding' – and that is what happened. Further it went into the river, accompanied by the rest of the bike and its rider.

There I stood, up to my waist in water – it was not deep, though of course I could not know this. I called to Bob but he had gone on. A boat was passing and I asked the pilot to tell the cyclist ahead that his friend was in the river.

Bob returned and helped me out of the water. 'Sorry I missed that', he said, 'I'd have taken a picture of it.'

'Do you want me to go back in again so that you can photograph the scene?'

I was very wet indeed and had not, foolishly, brought much clothing – and what I had was now soaked. We decided to take a detour into the city of Leicester and go to a shop. I found a t-shirt in a branch of somewhere like Marks and Spencers.

'Oh, nice choice,' said the girl in her West Midlands voice. 'Have you come in specially?'

'No, I just fell in the river.'

This caused her some amusement. 'Ow, you're the first person to tell me that this morning.'

It was worth falling in just to hear this.

We found our lodgings and I placed everything on a radiator; by the morning everything, including the camera, was dry.

Much of life has produced richness far beyond anything I might have imagined since then. Our three sons have been a wonderful and widely different bundle of infantry, at first as children and now as men. They all attended St Ignatius, all did pretty well though not outstandingly so, all worked much better than I did, probably under the influence of their mother, all survived the pastoral care of their father, all made good friends without holding on much to them, all are good at making friends anyway, all passed A-levels far better than I did – not difficult – all went to university and studied Arts degrees, all achieved a 2:1, as I did ultimately, all in their different ways have moved on to reasonable careers and all, as I write, remain employed.

The subjects they studied at A-level covered English, History, Politics and Art, and their degrees were in either Politics or English. Moreover, they seem to maintain thoughtful and cheerful characters, continue to be good talkers, independent thinkers and their own personalities. These aspects they have in common. Moreover, as far as I know, they remain on good terms with each other most of the time, though I cannot be certain of that. Above all, they all, in different ways, keep sound contact with both of their parents in spite of everything that has happened between us and I admire them for that. Of course, their parents' relationship is a different story and needs further development beyond the mention of choirs and cycling. They are pretty incisive in their judgements and entirely prepared to undertake anything needed to support especially their mother, challenging though that may sometimes be, and to raise more than an eyebrow over their father's approach to life.

Then there are the grandchildren. Tom and Sharmila have Nadia and Dillan, both watchful and bubbling in their different ways. I spend too little time with them, partly because travelling is difficult at the best of times – three hours each way to Dorking and back on a good day – and more so in the midst of this pestilence by which we are currently enveloped. Alex is the easiest to meet because he lives in North London and we can use the trains to devise meetings between there and Hertford. Ben and Tanja have the two children, Eliza and Chloe, but they live in Finland. When they were in Brussels, I went over a couple of times to see them but it has become more difficult and I cannot see any immediate prospect of getting over to the Arctic Circle.

Now to marital matters. For as long as I was still working, I would return home late and get on with things needing attention. There were things not quite right, unfortunately, but I was shrugging and resigned over them and assumed that, having committed myself to them, that was that for as long as breath continued to pass my lips. I did enjoy life a great deal but especially at school.

When I retired life changed. My wife once said that she had imagined my retirement would mean that we would be travelling here and there, visiting interesting places. Unfortunately, it was not like that. Being thrown together for longer periods, our differences became obvious.

By that time too, I had joined lots of choirs, especially the U3A choir in Hertford and the Barbershop septet arising from it. Before that it was the Ware Choral Society, for which I would cycle off to Ware every week in all weathers to learn and to sing under the conductor, Julian Williamson.

The U3A choirs were run by a lady with whom I found a lot in common, in terms of intellect and humour, as well as interests. The turning point came when she wrote to us to say that she was going to be away because of, she wrote, a 'sygmoidoscopy', as I have mentioned before. This misspelling drew us into lengthy correspondence and further exchanges.

The overlap came when my wife and I and I went to Provence. When we were there, she told me as we sat by a river near Avignon that she knew this would be our last holiday – I can't remember what drew us into that conversation. I had not advertised the situation but it had gradually become obvious over a few years. An account of the thinking and talking throughout that time would be worth the memory but it has all gone. Fairly conventional and predictable, I guess.

Somewhere in my papers there is a verse running roughly as follows:

An elderly fellow in France
Regretted he hadn't the chance
For the love of his life
Instead of his wife
To be there in Provence en vacances.

This was written in French first. That is how it was *'Un vieillard ...'* no, I can't recall it.

When we returned to England, it was not long before I found another address, in Hertford. Anthea Slate, a former colleague and current friend, a lady who had done us many favours when the children were little, carting them about here and there when hospital visits were needed, had asked me if I would join the volunteers to help at the new Methodist café in Hertford, Oasis – just one shift a week. Attached to the church as well was Ron Doragh. Anthea was well aware of our unhappy domestic situation, knew that I had to leave, knew that Ron had a room in his house. He offered, I moved, sending many of my books, for which there would be no room, into storage.

Meanwhile, we had sold our Hoddesdon house, split the proceeds and each bought a flat to let out, I in Hertford, she in Dorking.

Since then, I have moved once again and now live with *l'amour de ma vie* here in Bengeo, and have done so for perhaps nine years.

It is a cliché for men to leave their wives for a younger woman. I left my wife for an older woman.

That is the way life has developed. There remain of course many questions but it is not part of my remit to answer any more. Perhaps the observation of a mutual friend who has known us both very well, in different contexts, is apt. She told me a couple of years ago that it was inevitable and that we had done the right thing.

A few years ago, perhaps, when it was obviously all wrong, we tried to sort it all out by going to a marriage guidance counsellor. We made the appointment, arrived at the right time and were open-minded as to the outcome, as we knew it was crucial. The counsellor did not arrive. There is again no point in speculating on what might have happened if he or she had attended the rendezvous. We could write a story in which a meeting took place, an hour of discussion occurred, cards were put on the table, every aspect of the marriage was thrashed out and thought through, both of us were compelled to return to where we started and revive what we meant then; or we could write another narrative in which the same discussion disclosed, after the realities were revealed, that there was no way back. The reality is that no such meeting ever happened and we took the path we did without anyone's intervention.

Most times I ask about my wife's life and attitude I receive positive reports; though it is also clear that this is not strictly true because she is not well, in one or two ways. Naturally I would blame nobody, least of all the boys, for regarding me with anger or contempt – probably the former – mostly because, in different ways, they are carrying a weight which it was never designed that they should have to bear.

Even so, I hope that this account will have clarified the way that life has developed. Of course, the thoughtful reader will have still a number of questions to raise, in particular about the future possibilities for all parties.

Enough words.

AWH

****

ABOUT THE AUTHOR

'AWH'- thus he always signs himself - spent much of his life teaching Classics in two boys' schools, one in Devon, the other in Enfield, until he retired from the profession in 2011. As well as classroom teaching, he became a leading pastoral figure among pupils from 11 to 18. He has been a school governor in several schools in Hertfordshire, primary and secondary. A keen walker and cyclist, he has unpublished journals of a number of his escapades as well as this much longer journey.